T0319199

Stifled Justice in Cameroon: Detained for Six Years Without Judgement

Rose Chia Fonchingong

Langaa Research & Publishing CIG
Mankon, Bamenda

Publisher
Langaa RPCIG
Langaa Research & Publishing Common Initiative Group
P.O. Box 902 Mankon
Bamenda
North West Region
Cameroon
Langaagrp@gmail.com
www.langaa-rpcig.net

Distributed in and outside N. America by African Books Collective
orders@africanbookscollective.com
www.africanbookscollective.com

ISBN: 9956-763-76-4

DISCLAIMER
All views expressed in this publication are those of the author and do not
necessarily reflect the views of Langaa RPCIG.

Chapter One

M y story is one that starts with a lot of joy and ends in... I want to say sadness. But sadness is not quite the word, because at the moment I'm not really that sad person again.

The problem started when I was appointed as provincial coordinator for the HIV and AIDS control team for the South-West Region. This appointment was made by Urban Olangena Awono, the former Minister of Public Health, sometime in June 2004.

For one reason or the other, I realised that the person I was going to replace did not want to quit the post and kept me waiting until September.

I took that as normal, because I was still holding another post as the District Medical Officer for Limbe Health District. So it really did not disturb me, since I was busy.

Finally, on the 12ᵗʰ of October, this person I was going to replace left and handed over to me.

It is during the handing over that I realised there was a problem, that even my immediate collaborators and the health authorities did not want me to take the post. The Delegate for Health at the time thought he could influence my replacement. They had asked me to stay put because they wanted to see whether I could be replaced.

While I waited perplexed by the delay, the minister had called to find out whether the handing over had taken place. He ordered that I should take over the post with immediate effect. Then they gave in and hurriedly allowed me to take over.

Immediately I took over the post, the delegate again hurriedly went ahead and replaced me as district medical officer for the Limbe health district.

It was not normal. I was appointed by a prime ministerial decision and the delegate could not just replace me. So he asked me to go and hand over. I said before handing over I have to make hierarchy know and address the situation because anything can happen and I will be held responsible.

I wrote officially to the minister telling him the delegate had appointed somebody to replace me. When the Minister got the correspondence, he was very furious. He called that delegate to order and asked him to cancel his appointment decision because he did not have any right to appoint a district medical officer given the fact that, he was cancelling a prime ministerial decision.

The delegate yielded. He kept me there and the already tense situation aggravated. In my own office whenever I gave orders to any collaborator there was always some resistance. According to them, I did not have any knowledge on the functioning of the project and they were not ready to make things easy for me. Not only was there overt animosity, they went to the extent of writing against me to hierarchy of the national control programme for the fight against HIV/AIDS, and even to the World Bank office in Yaoundé, the funding body of the programme.

Fortunately I had alerted the minister that since my appointment to that post of coordinator of the Provincial Technical Group (PTG) for HIV/AIDS in the South-West, the South-Westerners did not like my presence in that office. I could see no reason why they didn't like me beyond the fact that I am from the North-West region and they think that that position is a position for the South-Westerners. This is what I told the minister when he inquired.

The minister told me to stay quiet and I stayed quiet. This helped me because any letter of complaint about me that he saw he just put it aside. He knew that there was a problem, I had already warned him.

When the delegate realised that he could not succeed by using my collaborators, he turned around and mounted the partners with whom he worked against me. These were presidents of the NGOs involved in the project. So every time I called for these people to tender for an activity, they always thought that I was cheating them out of the funding. If they had to carry out an activity for 1000 000 FCFA, and I asked them to sign a contract to be paid in two instalments as stipulated in the manual of procedures, they would complain to the point of insinuating that I was being too strict and stingy with the money, while elsewhere others were paying ten million francs for more or less the same activity that I was contracting them to undertake. It was clear that they wanted the money but not the work. That didn't go down well with me. I am a no nonsense leader. Whenever I went out to supervise what they were doing, they did not like it. They started writing negative reports about me. I was adamant. I told them: 'Until you do what you are supposed to do, I will not pay.'

Another opposition group against me was quickly growing. This was the purported representatives of civil society. These people openly told me I was occupying the post of a South-Westerner. So whenever I sublet any community mobilisation and sensitisation to them and the job was not well done, and I refused to order payment to them, it became a bone of contention. They also started writing to the Governor of the province and even to the Minister of Public Health. There were instances where I was accused by these NGO leaders of taking funds meant for the South-West and giving these funds to the North Westerners. They could not disabuse themselves of the expectation that I should pay them higher than was stated by the programme.

3

I had a lot of problems with the people around me and my collaborators in the programme. My personal file at the level of Yaoundé was not a clean file, because people kept on writing against me. And a lot of them even reportedly went as far as to write to the presidency of the country.

One lady came and told me that they are going to remove me from this office one day at one o'clock news. She had a contract to go mobilise, sensitise and educate a community but she thought she was going for a pleasure trip. A dead whale had just been washed to shore and this lady went and abandoned the work she was doing and went and climbed on the whale and started snapping pictures on the whale and that was her report. Unfortunately for her, I had gone to the field to supervise her at the time. I told her that despite her report I had indicators which I expected to see inside it. So, she wrote to the governor and a lot of other people around. I guess she is one of the political movers and shakers around here presently. So when she wrote, the governor wrote asking me to pay. I wrote and told the governor I was not going to pay because the job was not done. He convened me to his office and with threats he ordered me to pay because the lady who issued the complaint was a political figure. Being a technician who was results oriented I did not pay and this act was considered as arrogance and disturbance on my part.

Everything was playing out beautifully as planned by my antagonists. Soon, everybody in Yaoundé knew that the working environment of the provincial technical group for the fight against HIV/AIDS in the South-West was not the best.

My immediate boss and the permanent secretary for the national AIDS control committee saw all the complaints written against me. He even started believing in them until I told him one day that every week he should expect to see somebody in his office coming to complain about me. Since I

4

did the job expected of me he had no other choice than to believe me.

Towards the end of 2006 we were informed that a control team from the higher state control was going to come and control the programme without stating the exact dates of the mission. After six months of waiting without them coming we thought they had called off the provincial phase of the control. Then sometime in May 2007, I remember it was on a Friday, and I was somewhere in Manyu Division on supervision. I was called by one of my colleagues who was heading the tuberculosis programme and told that some people were coming from Yaoundé to control the HIV and AIDS programme. I said I am used to controls, there is nothing strange. Why should these people be calling for me instead of sending an official letter to let me know their schedule? Why should she be the one calling? I said anyway this is Friday; I am rounding up my supervision in the field. I will be in Buea on Monday.

Immediately she dropped the phone, some strange person called from Douala. I knew it was a call from Douala because it was a number from a fixed phone. So when the person called, I answered and he screamed: 'Madame, when I call you answer!'

I was surprised and asked him how he came about the conclusion that I didn't want to answer him? He went on to say, 'They've told me that you are a very stubborn person, so just be very careful'.

I said, 'I am in the field sir, if you called my office without a reply, it is because I am in the field and I want to believe you already called the Provincial Delegate for Health and he must have informed you of my whereabouts. He was the one who placed me on this mission.'

My explanation did little to calm him down. He threatened, threatened, threatened.

I asked him not to threaten me before the control. I told him that I was going to be in my office upon his arrival.

This was on Friday. With this information I informed my team members that we were cutting short our mission because controllers expected all of us in the office on Monday.

On Monday morning, I asked my collaborators to get all their documents ready.

Around 11 o'clock a four man team of controllers came to my office. On arrival and after greeting and receiving them, the Head of mission turned around and said, 'She's not as bad as we thought'.

I said, 'What do you mean by I am not as bad as you thought?'

He said, 'The impression we got is that you are a very bad person.'

Naturally, I am somebody who laughs a lot. So when they came in I was laughing.

I asked the head of mission whether he was the one who threatened me over the phone. I asked him what I could have done to receive so many threats.

He introduced himself as Mr Bayoi, and then introduced the other team members and informed me that one was absent and will be joining them later. She was absent because she was giving classes in the university of Douala.

He went ahead to present the method of the control to me and my staff.

He told me he wanted an office, a computer, a car and he wanted all their phones to be credited with airtime and that I should take care of their hotel bills.

When he finished, I informed him that we had just two vehicles. One was presently not very good and I could not hand over the service car I was using to him.

He said that in the absence of a care, I had to provide fuel to the team.

I told him that I did not have fuel to give them because the monthly allocation was already finished.

Concerning crediting their telephones with airtime, it was out of the question because the monthly allocation for the whole office was 100, 000 FCFA and we had already distributed it.

Then, after threatening, he turned around and said I should now ensure that they are satisfied, because he is the one who sent the FEICOM people, Odongdong and others, to prison. We have to be very careful the way we treat him, he warned.

He turned around and told me that I should take him to a hotel. I called for my accountant and asked him, since he was in charge of finances, to look through his budget to find out if there is a budgetary line to pay hotel bills for controllers.

Of course, there wasn't.

So I told the accountant to make sure that the team of controllers had coffee every day because at least it was budgeted for. I asked him to look for 50 000 FCFA to make sure they had something to eat during coffee breaks.

Mr Bayoi was not happy with the arrangement and he asked me to make all the necessary arrangements to get some money for his team because the Minister of Public Health was not cooperating with the mission team. I asked him whether he had a letter from the minister instructing me to take care of them. With such a letter, I would carry out the instructions without grumbling.

I told him that I could not assist them out of my salary. I was very frank with him, and I told him that being on mission their mission allowances should have taken care of them.

After this introduction, the team requested to see the Provincial Delegate for Health and I conveyed them to the delegate's office. They presented and explained their terms of reference to the delegate.

The position of provincial delegate for health conferred on him the role of general supervisor of all health programmes in the province. In the case of the Provincial AIDS Control Committee, he was even a signatory to some bank accounts. He immediately started complaining that now when it is control he is involved but during management of finances, he sees money passing over his head.

This had always been a bone of contention with him because he did not understand why the funds for the HIV/AIDS control programme were not managed by him. It escaped him completely that I had not made the rules. All I did was implement the regulations in place. I told him that he had access to that money. All he had to do was to ask for the cheque book to be brought to him for signature but with tangible proof that the funds will be used for legitimate HIV/AIDS control activities. I asked him to stop complaining to these people as if my office was using the money without his approval.

To pacify most of these bosses, they were given monthly allowance of 100, 00FCFA in the form of telephone credits or fuel bonds. They were still not satisfied because as they constantly said there is a lot of money in that program and that woman is eating a lot.

At this juncture I left the team with the delegate and went back to my office.

The control proper started immediately. A team member was sent to control my office. I had earlier presented all my collaborators to the control team. The team requested that we should each present to them our posting decisions and to tell them how long each of us had worked in the programme. During this encounter I also told them that all inquiries concerning finances should be addressed to the accountant. Their control method was to request for information through what they called 'demande de renseignement'. As the name suggests, they asked me to explain why such and such a thing happened. From this I deduced that unlike previous financial controllers who would only work with the accountant these wanted to get everyone involved. I called the attention of all my collaborators and that of the accountant in particular because I realised that these controllers were not really interested in our performances, although that is what they originally stated in their Terms of Reference (TOR). They were more interested in controlling finances. I asked the accountant to get all financial information ready.

At one point I even referred them to the manual of procedure, telling them that the accountant is supposed to answer to all questions concerning finances. I countersigned cheques and bank transfers only at the accountant's approval. So, if he does not approve, I cannot sign the cheque. Neither can the delegate sign the cheque.

At the beginning of the control, bank transfers, printouts of all the financial transactions for the period and bank statements of the different accounts of the programme were collected from the accountant. The team then used the information contained in these financial documents as basis for their 'demandes de renseignements'

When an inquiry concerned an activity, we replied as a team. But what concerned finances, I let the accountant deal with it.

Three days after working with the control team, I obtained permission to go for an interview in Yaoundé that had been postponed several times and this was the last chance I had. It was a two day permission, and I hoped to be back to continue work with the control team.

The evening I returned from Yaounde, I learnt that the control team had left. The female member of the control team reportedly delayed in Douala had joined them in the meantime. He was told she was very furious that I was not around. And because of that she went to the accountant's office and without looking at what she was taking away, collected files of financial documents and other papers. She was haphazard and indiscriminate in what she collected.

It seems as if before leaving the team held a meeting with the accountant and the provincial delegate. Up till today, I don't know the outcome of that meeting. I don't know what was said in that meeting. All I know is that when I came back, the accountant changed. He was no longer the very accountant I knew.

When he told me that the lady controller had collected files from his office, I asked him if that was possible that somebody could enter his office and collect financial documents without him making photocopies. He told me he had no time to make photocopies. I asked him to go to Yaoundé and bring back the documents.

Within the month that followed, three 'demandes de renseignements' were sent to me concerning some financial transactions which were inside the files the lady had collected. In the inquiries, I was requested to give explanations concerning gaps in the justification documents of activities that were in the files. In reply, I told them that I could not even give any answers to the questions they were asking me because they had collected all the originals which were in the accountant's office. Secondly, they were asking about financial matters and I had earlier on told them that they should address all the questions concerning finances to the accountant. I could not answer about any records of the accountant.

I even asked the accountant to reply to the queries, which he told me he did.

The weakness on my part is that I believed him. I did not crosscheck to confirm that he had sent the reply to the controllers. I thought everything was over. Until one day when in Bamenda, I met my colleague in the North West province, and she wanted to know what happened between me and the controllers when they were in Buea. She told me that while in Bamenda, they were very angry with me and threatened that I was going to see.

This made me to call Mr Bayoi, the head of the control mission, to find out why he went around talking about me with threats to other people? He said 'No, Madam, there's no problem, just answer the various queries that we sent to you. If you send the answers, there will be no problem.'

I replied that my accountant had already sent the replies. Mr Bayoi said he had not seen the replies, because there were lots of papers and at that time he had not yet worked on those for the South-West Province.

On arrival in Buea, I asked the accountant with insistence if he had sent the replies and repeated what Mr Bayoi said to me. He told me he sent the replies.

After this I just forgot about the control and their queries and I went about my normal duties until the 31st of March 2008.

I can always remember that it was a Monday when I went to the office. That morning I heard over the news that they had arrested Mr Olangena, the former Minister of Public Health and Mr Abah Abah, former Minister of Finance.

All the staff of the PTG were tired because we had spent a hectic week supervising activities in the field. That news of these arrests was like another docking in frozen water for everyone. At about 9 o'clock that morning, somebody called and told me that they have arrested the permanent secretary for the Central Technical Group. A call to the head office in Yaoundé confirmed that Dr Fezeu, former permanent Secretary of the AIDS Control Programme and Dr Okalla, the permanent secretary for the malaria control programme had been arrested.

Then the colleague at the Yaoundé end of the phone asked whether I had any problem during the control. I jokingly asked if there was somebody who did not have problems with the controllers. Why should the South-West be so particular? He explained that he saw the name of South-West on a list.

I said 'No, I am not sure that you saw very well.'

Whatever the case, I called the accountant, Mr Thomas Ngiumpack, to again find out where he kept the copies of the replies he forwarded to the controllers, because he was no longer working with us and the new accountant could not find it. Mr Nguipack's contract ended in December 2007. He was now working for a private accounting firm, the funders of our programme having insisted that they did not want their money to be controlled by civil servants.

Mr Nguimpack asked us to search in the office.

When I think back I remember that in February, a president of an NGO, Mme Omam, being a friend, had called and said she wanted to meet with me. I invited her to my house but she preferred to meet with me on some neutral ground.

According to her she wanted to tell me something but not at home.

I therefore asked that we meet at OIC in Great Soppo. At this point she offered an invitation for lunch and then we will discuss the issue over lunch. I told her I was bringing a friend. I became very suspicious. So before going, I took Dr Irene Anyangwe along. I explained the situation to Dr Anyangwe.

I liked Mme Omam. She was very friendly and hardworking and I helped take her NGO off the ground, I gave her many recommendations. Prior to this incident, I realised that she was behaving funny towards me.

Immediately she saw Dr Anyangwe, her countenance completely changed. She did not want to talk again. When I asked her concerning the issue we had to discuss; she said she just wanted me to be careful. I should know that I am working in a position where people don't really like me.

I said, 'What is the problem? Tell me.'

Dr Anyangwe turned around and said, 'Madam, if there is a problem, tell her. She is my sister and my friend. If there is anything, any precautions that you want her to take in particular, let us know.'

Mme Omam made a lot of noise but said nothing in particular.

Monday 31st of March 2008 had already started very badly with many apprehensions. Work had to continue. There was a meeting at the delegation of health. I went and attended. For one reason or the other, I could not keep still in the meeting. So I left to carry out other duties. I was arranging for AIDS orphans to be taken care of and this took me to the Central Pharmacy to arrange with the manager on how we could put in place a scheme to provide medicines to orphans went to the hospital.

It was during our discussion that, four policemen arrived. They greeted and asked for Dr Chia Rose Fonchingong and I said I was the one. Then they said that they were there to take me to the provincial delegation of national security for questioning. They would not even allow me to take my handbag from the car.

Chapter Two

On arrival at the police station, I asked the Police commissioner who arrested me what must have gone wrong. The only thing he told me is, 'Madam, I am following instructions, but it should be in connection with the arrest of your former minister Olangena, and three other permanent secretaries in Yaoundé, your name is on the list.'

When I sat there, it dawned on me that somebody had warned me earlier on that morning that they saw the name of South-West on the list and in connection with the controllers of the higher state control.

At least the police permitted me to use my phone. I called the new accountant and he had not found anything. I again called the former accountant and I asked him to tell us where exactly to look for the reply in the office. I did not want to disclose to him that I was in police custody, but I think already, the other collaborators told him I had been arrested, because he stopped taking my calls. From that day up till today, I have never spoken to nor seen Mr Nguimpack. I became so desperate that I even called his wife and I asked her to plead with her husband to come and sort out where he kept the reply to the query because I was now in police custody. The woman made some noise as if she was going to do something and later on her own phone went dead. I could no longer get in touch with them.

I called my husband, and my friend Dr Anyangwe, and they were permitted to see me. It is then that Dr Anyangwe reminded me of the famous lunch that we had with Mrs Omam. The Delegate for health came. I don't think he uttered a word. He looked at me and left. This is someone who during one occasion had boasted to my husband that just one word to the right ear would have me removed from office. Now he saw it happening in a bigger way than he had probably imagined.

At about 6 pm, I was transferred to the famous judicial police in Yaoundé, where everybody suspected of committing any hideous crime in Cameroon is kept in custody.

We arrived at about midnight. The situation was so surreal. In my mind, I had not integrated the fact that the situation was serious. I thought I was conveyed to Yaounde for questioning, then to be set free when they got the facts right.

What struck me though is that on arrival, my colleagues were locked up in the common cell with all types of people. Then they asked me to go inside. When they opened the door of the cell, a strong stench left. I shouted in a loud voice that I was not going inside a smelly room. I think they took pity on me because I was pushed into what looked like an office when another door was opened.

As I entered, I saw two human forms stretched out on the floor. On a closer look, I realised that one of them was former Minister of Finance, Mr Ababa Polycarp, and next to him was the former Minister of Public Health, Olangena.

I assume that they were sleeping, because none of them acknowledged my presence.

A policeman gave me a mattress to sleep on, after warning me that it was a big favour because I was supposed to sleep on the floor.

I don't think I slept that night although by day break, I was taken to a very filthy toilet to clean up. I had no option, I had to clean up.

When I came back into our cell, the two former dignitaries of this country still lay face down whispering to each other with very dejected looks on their faces.

Around midday Mr Olangena finally turned his head and looked at me very closely and exclaimed, 'Dr Chia! What are you doing here?'

I told him I was brought in the previous night. And he wanted to know what must have happened. I told him since I was arrested nobody has told me anything. All I know is that they told me that it is in connection with the control from the Higher State Control mission.

During the day I was conveyed to the office of the Delegate for National Security. When the man saw me, his expression was like 'Is this you?!!'

I said, 'What have I done?'

He said, 'No, I am just surprised, because when I hear the millions that you are supposed to have embezzled, when I look at you, you don't look like the millions.

I said, 'Embezzled millions for what?'

He said, 'Anyway, we are going to tell you later on.'

Day two in police custody. Mr Abah Abah had a heart attack inside the cell. It was something else because his own son who is a medical doctor came to take care of his father and nobody will allow him in. I heard the police arguing about it but firm instructions were given that they were going to assign a cardiologist to attend to him. Since the state did not have a cardiologist handy, his personal doctor did an electrocardiogram on him. But they needed a neutral doctor from the central hospital to assess him. This doctor, a cardiologist, came and refused to assist Mr Abah Abah.

That's when I realised that the problem was not as easy as I thought. I witnessed a scenario where a former minister of Cameroon was very ill and a medical doctor who had taken the Hippocratic Oath, a specialist for that matter, refused to take care of him. Fortunately the family put a lot of pressure and the next day Abah Abah was transferred to the hospital.

This incident made me there and then to take a decision to be strong because where I was sitting I had neither money nor the power. I could only rely on God. I had not eaten for two days, that's when I started eating.

On the fourth day, they called for me to some part of that judicial police office. I met with two people who said they were investigators. My finger prints and pictures were taken and my face was photographed from every angle. What you see in criminal investigation films is what happens in real world. I was then assigned to two investigators who formerly presented the charges against me. I was accused of embezzling 508, 819, 000FCFA from the Cameroon government through the Provincial Technical Group for HIV/AIDS for the South-West as follows:

- One hundred and fifty seven million, five hundred and twenty six thousands (157, 526, 000FCFA) they claimed was spent without justification;
- One million two hundred and forty nine thousands (1, 249, 000FCFA) were paid out to different people, then appending their identity card numbers and without signatures;
- Over Three Hundred and forty thousands (340, 000, 000FCFA.) was transferred from the account of the provincial technical group to the account of other beneficiaries and they wanted to know who they were and what they did with the money;
- Two Hundred and eight million (208, 000, 000 FCFA) – was paid to local AIDS control committees against instructions from hierarchy – i.e. hierarchy had asked me to stop these payments and I went ahead and continued payments. Concerning this money in particular, when the controllers came, I explained to them and I actually gave them all the justification documents proving the fact that hierarchy

18

had asked me to continue payment and that it was a communication problem.

After these charges were read, I told them how the project was organised according to World Bank procedures. I told them that I was not supposed to be in charge of financial justifications. I told them that what they wanted from me were financial justifications and it is the accountant who was in charge. I was informed that if I could not present the justification documents, then I was going to stay there and answer in court. They then insisted that I needed a lawyer for further interrogations.

It was an ordeal getting a lawyer. Not being based in Yaounde, I did not know any lawyer in particular. My husband and relatives moved from one legal chamber to the other and every time the lawyers heard the type of case they asked for ten percentage of the amount I was accused of embezzling. To them if you are accused of embezzling such an amount it means you can afford at least 10% for their fees.

Finally, my niece who had practised in a law firm pleaded with a young lawyer to take the case. That was mistake number one and another story concerning my encounters with lawyers.

On day eight in police custody we were taken to court. I experienced the anger of Cameroonians on that day. The police bus that transported us to court had to be heavily guarded because there was a mob action and demonstration just in front of the judicial police. They had gotten wind that the people who economically brought Cameroon to its feet were about to be taken to court. Immediately the bus moved, they started throwing stones at us and calling us thieves. At the level of the cathedral and the post office roundabout, they had to completely stop traffic and bar the way to pedestrians. By then, every Cameroonian believed that we were all guilty.

I don't know why they took us there, because after sitting in a hallway for about two hours we were carried back to the police station. At one instance, I even shouted, 'Please can you tell me what is happening?! I don't want to be sitting here blindly'. The reply was a lot of legal terms that I didn't understand.

On the ninth day, the same process as the previous evening was repeated. But this time they made sure that we left about 10pm. I had never had anything to do with the police, not to talk of the courts.

That evening, when my sister came visiting, I did not know that I should have asked her to hang around the police station and see what was going to happen.

At about 9 pm a female police officer asked me to arrange my things because I was going to be transferred that night. When I asked her about my destination, she said to better quarters. She gave me her phone to call my relatives. Being that late, none of them could come back to the police station. So they told me that they will see about the things the next day. That night out of eight who were held in what became known as the Olangena and others case; two were released and the rest of us signed the reprimand warrant transferring us to the Kondegui Central prison in Yaoundé.

Chapter Three

Kondengui is called the eleventh province or region of Cameroon, because you are inside Cameroon but you are not in Cameroon. Immediately after arrest, your national identity card is confiscated. You are as the francophone would put it – 'le detenu'. They don't care whatever status you had in life, you are 'le detenu'. And anybody, from the least warder to the highest can treat you the way they want.

We arrived the prison at about 1 am on the 10th of April 2008. We sat in an open court yard for what seemed like hours in the cold with no one telling us anything. At one point, we were ushered into an office and a prison administrator received us and introduced himself as the 'regisseur de la prison'.

At about 2am we were finally assigned to different quarters of the prison. On arrival into quarter five – the female quarters, there was a big crowd, a welcome party of women screaming. Some of them were beating their buckets and everything they could lay hands upon. It was a loud noise. You can imagine that I was already under the trauma of being in prison at 2am in the morning and led along a dark corridor and all of sudden a gate was opened and I was ordered to go in just to be received by that party.

I wanted to turn around and run out of the gate but it was already closed. There were three of us. I was accompanied by two other ladies who had been arrested in connection with Minister Abah Abah. In the noise some shouted, 'Asoyah! Asoyah!' Some added: 'These are the people who have brought Cameroon down to its knees. You thought you were the untouchables'. Others invited us to forget about the ministers with whom we had been escorted to prison: 'Since you came

21

with those ministers, just forget about them, because now they belong to us.'

I told myself: These are criminals who are calling me a criminal.

The warders had to go and push them aside to let us go in.

We were presented to a lady prisoner inside a prison room and this woman was called 'le commandant'. The prison also has its own order and hierarchy, not only among the prison administrators, but also among prisoners. The commandant questioned us and wrote down the information inside a register. The information she collected was on questions like: What are you here for? How old are you? And where do you come from? She got some information from us. After which she assigned us to different rooms in the quarter.

She kept me in her own room. I did not know keeping me in her room was a big honour. She asked one small girl to host me on her bed. I spent my first night on the top bunk of a bed that could barely contain one person. But this particular bunk bed was a whole house. It contained boxes, food and dishes. It was a five spring bed. That is where I went. On that bed I could not sit; short as I am. I could not sit up straight on the bed. When I forgot and sat up straight, I always hit my head on the floor of the bed above. To sit up the angle between my torso and hips had to be at least 150 degrees.

Normally it's a three place bunk bed. There is the top, the middle and then the bottom, depending on the height of the roof. I'm sure if the roof were much higher, the bunk bed would even go up to four stairs.

In my last year in prison, I had the privilege to be assigned to a bunk bed which had just two stairs and thanks to this I had more space and so I could use my bunk to hid things. The space between your bed and bunk above you was enclosed shelves fitted on the wall. You create space for your small TV;

we used the smallest size of television, because the bigger ones couldn't fit. Under the TV, you create space for your radio or whatever you have. On the sides, you put the shelves for your clothes. There were no prison uniforms. The Cameroon government cannot afford to clothe all the prisoners.

That first night in prison, I had just stretched out on the bed when at about 4 a.m., I heard a noise coming from the cell. Good God... rats. I've never seen rats like that. Rats playing, a couple, kissing themselves. Yes, the rats will stand and kiss themselves and clap their hands and... that was the first time. I screamed. I could not believe what I was seeing.

Everybody started laughing. They were expecting that, and when they heard me screaming, everybody burst out and started laughing.

I said, 'Have you people not seen what is happening there?'

They said, 'Madame, don't disturb us. If you have just come, don't disturb us. We are tired, we want to sleep.'

I spent the rest of the night watching rats at play.

There are a lot of stories about those rats. When we put rat poison, the rats will disappear for two days and on the third day you see them coming back. We knew all the different rats. There are stories of people who claimed to have seen some of the rats with chains on the legs. These rats, these particular rats, they did not drink just any water. They only drank bottled mineral water like Tangui water. If you filled tap water in a bottle and you placed it by any mineral water these rats could identify which was mineral water. They never pierce the bottle of the normal tap water to drink; they only pierced the bottle of the mineral water to drink. These are rats that drank eggs. One day, somebody brought me a tray of eggs and I placed it on top of a shelf and I was there happy, thinking that I had eggs. I think after four or five days, something started smelling in my bed. On searching, I realised that rats had drank all the eggs. They had pierced holes and sucked out the eggs without breaking the shells, and all the thirty eggs went that way. Vampire rats!

One night, I was sleeping and felt this sharp pain as if someone had injected my big toe. As I abruptly woke up from sleep with a scream, I saw blood oozing out of my toe.

The older inmates started laughing and told me that the rats had taken a very long time to welcome me. In those days, it was normal reception for new inmates. Real vampire rats!

These were very big rats. Rats that fought with owls!

One night I was sitting outside, everybody had gone in and I was not feeling well, so I was sitting outside on the corridor. An owl flew down trying to catch a baby rat and one giant rat jumped up to get the owl also. The owl flew and perched on top of the roof and was looking at that rat on the ground. The rats were not afraid of us. They fed in front of us as if we were roommates.

Our cockroaches were also not the normal type. We don't have that big specie of cockroaches we usually see in homes around. Ours are the very small type. In Kondengui the big type of cockroaches seem to be uncomfortable and have made way for the army of small cockroaches. They are thousands of time, and they bite like hell. These were cockroaches that only fed on human flesh. Their speciality was to feed on the blood of fair skinned women, mostly those of them who bleach their skin.

At one time we invited Reverend Men of God to pray over the quarters because we believed that the presence of the rats and cockroaches was demonic. The quarters were disinfected regularly but the situation never changed. The rats used our beds to breed. You would be lying on your bed thinking that you are the only occupant just to discover one day when you opened your mattress that rats have delivered under.

The story is that Kondengui prison was built on a graveyard. Rumour has it that the people buried there have been coming back and terrorising inmates. Even some prisoners are said to have turned into rats. I never saw that one with the chain on the leg, but a lot of women said they saw it. They confessed that they saw a rat with a chain on the leg. That particular rat was like a prisoner who used to come around and go around disturbing women.

We sleep with lights on. The doors are all open. The room is like six metres by eight. Normally, that room is supposed to take 16 persons. There are six bunk beds of three places in each room. But when the place is overcrowded, people sleep on the floor. When it was overcrowded, it took at least thirty persons. And when you want to go out, you trample on others.

At day break, I went to fetch water for my bath, and realised that only one tap, dropping a small stream of water, was serving almost one hundred and five women. There was a long line of buckets waiting to fetch water from that tap. You dare not touch any body's bucket; that was as good as inviting a fight.

That morning, I discovered that the insults of the previous night had just been kept waiting for an opportunity to vent it out on me. Immediately I approached the tap, someone beckoned to me to bring my bucket. Then this tomboy of girl, I later learnt was a hardened criminal, came and removed the bucket and threw it away.

It became a common sight that those of them who had been in and out of the prison several times will wait for you by the tap just to insult you. When you go there to fetch water, they will just bring their bucket with all the dirt and put in front of your bucket to make sure that the dirt drops inside your bucket. If you dared to open your mouth and talk, then you were inviting insults and even a physical fight. I did not want to believe that this was happening to me.

The commandant on my first day asked me look for somebody to take care of me like a servant or house-help. Since she had spent almost ten years in prison, she knew that the naughty prisoners were spoiling for a fight with me. They knew that in the outside world they could never have the opportunity of living and eating with a medical doctor in the same place. That is why the commandant warned me to search for someone to take care of me.

Before it actually dawned on me what the commandant meant, on the second day of my arrival in prison a girl who dressed and looked like a boy and who I heard had been in and out of prison since she was twelve years old was waiting for me at the tap.

During my stay in Kondengui, this boy-girl, nicknamed Joey, left and came back at least six times.

There are a lot of young people like Joey who started going to prison early. They don't know how to live outside again. Even when they are released, they always go and commit some crime, are arrested and brought back again. Joey has been in and out of prison until people have forgotten how to count.

On that morning, Joey was waiting for me at the tap. I did not know she had plans for me. I waited for my turn to fetch water. Just as I put my bucket to collect the water, Joey brought a dirty bucket, pushed mine aside. On impulse, I pushed away her bucket.

Oh God! Heaven broke loose. Joey carried a bucket of water and poured it on me. I was dragged away from there before I had retaliated. I was told she wanted me to retaliate for a fight to start.

The insults I heard, which were to become very common during my stay at Kondengui, were: 'Look at this thief! You are

26

the people who are making Cameroonians to be suffering. Look at you, a Medical doctor... instead of treating people, you go around stealing.'

This was still on day one, 10th April 2008. However, I had a bath that day and was immediately called by a warder to report to the main office 'GREFFE'. I arrived there and in an inhumane office they asked me to strip off my dress because a lady wardress was about to examine my body for any natural or permanent marks.

It was very humiliating because this was done in the presence of men.

This was followed by taking our finger prints and then the photo session. After the warder, came the turn of the health staff, to make enquiries concerning our medical history, and to physically examine us as well. Fortunately, the chief medical officer had worked with me in Buea, so I was given a better treatment here.

The interesting thing is that I was abandoned at the 'Greffe' I sat there expecting that the warder who accompanied me was going to take me back to the female quarters. But she did not show up. After sometime, I decided to look for my way back.

At the first gate, I was barred from going through because according to them only authorised persons could go into the inner court yard of the prison. I struggled to present myself as a prisoner and I was sent back. I eventually got back to my quarters.

Today I wonder why I did not think of just walking out of that place into the streets of Yaoundé. Can you imagine one of Biya's most valuable detainees being rejected?

My relatives eventually came with my mattress, clothes and toilet equipment after they went to the police station and were informed that we had been transferred to Kondengui.

The weeping was too much. When I was still at the police station, they had some hopes that I was going to be released. But now that I was in prison, it meant something else.

They didn't have the privilege to weep or converse with me for long. The chief warden in charge of the female quarters, Mr Aloua came and ordered them to leave, insisting that they could only see me for five minutes.

Immediately after we signed the reprimand warrant, instructions came that we were not supposed to have any visitors until further notice. So when my relatives came, I barely collected the items they brought and they were sent away.

Subsequently, there were instances when my visitors were just pushed away. I even remember an occasion when my husband visited and even before we could embrace each other we were separated. I was pushed inside like a recalcitrant child.

Chapter Four

The hygienic conditions of the female quarters in particular of Kondengui prison were deplorable. When I just got into prison, the latrine that had and still has just three toilet pots was all cracked. These three toilets, housed in three tiny cubicles of the latrine, had to serve over one hundred and fifty, and at times two hundred women. They were constantly blocked, because of the way they were used. There was no water most of the time and women who had never used a water system toilet, using it for the first time, they deposited just anything inside. There was manpower to clean the place alright, but you know the mentality of human beings, not to talk of the mentality of prisoners. Some deliberately made the place filthy, and took much joy from doing so. It was beyond horrible. I still develop goose pimples just thinking about this.

Fortunately, a religious organisation, that was doing some missionary work inside the prison, came to the assistance of the women and refurbished and modernised that toilet.

Fortune was on my side as well. I met a relative's husband who was into prison ministry, and he became a pillar of support to me in the early days of my imprisonment. He came right inside the female quarters, and through him, I could receive and send information to my relatives. He even introduced me to other pastors who assisted me as well.

I can always remember this incident when one of the pastors brought my very close friend, Dr Irene Anyangwe, right inside my prison cell. On this particular day I was feeling very frustrated and wondering what was going to happen to me, when I realised that somebody was standing by my bed.

There were times this pastor would come and pull me out of bed, when he realised I was not sitting in the court yard like other inmates. So on this famous Saturday morning when I saw his feet by the bed I thought he had come again for another counselling session.

I heard 'Maitre'. That is what Irene calls me.

All hell broke loose. I felt the blow. I would have loved to describe my living condition to her without allowing her to see where I was sleeping. Don't forget that I could not sit up on my bed and it had been covered with some rags to keep the rats out. My shame was the shock of her eyes.

Irene spent all the time of her visit weeping and the only thing she could say was to ask me what I was doing in this place.

I asked Irene how they managed to get her into prison and right into my room. The only way she could come right where I was could only have been through smuggling. That's how she came – as a preacher.

The presence of Irene in my prison cell healed a wound in me. From that day, I stopped crying, at least, the continuous crying of self-pity.

The prison inmates had been made to think that they were there to do menial work for the warders, who brought things like egusi to peel, ndole to be washed. Warders brought even their clothes for prisoners to wash.

The first day I turned down peeling egusi, I was told by the commandant, 'Madame, you have to peel it or you pay somebody to do it.'

I told her I was not going to peel it. Neither was I going to pay someone to do it. I told her that was something that I could not remember the last time that I did it in my own house and I was not going to do it for a warder.

The next instance was bitter leaf that was divided to all the female inmates to wash. I think this time I told them I was awaiting trial and not yet convicted. The work they wanted me to do was meant for prisoners, I insisted.

As punishment for refusing to do the menial jobs, I was asked to leave the bed. That small girl with whom I was sleeping had left the bed for me. They came and removed me from the bed and asked the small girl to go back on her bed. Respectful of my age, the girl accepted but later on went and looked for another place to sleep.

The humiliation was too much. I was repeatedly told to forget about what I used to be in the land of the free. In prison I had no identity. It's like they want to walk on you.

One day, I had just finished bathing and while I was dressing up in my cell, I was told that one of the chief warders was coming in with some visitors. I went inside the bed and pulled the blinds to completely conceal my presence as these people came right into the room. Under my cover my telephone started ringing. Telephones were illegal, but I had managed to smuggle in a cell phone. As I struggled to silence the telephone, a prisoner who accompanied the visitors, heard the sound of the telephone and she knew that I was inside.

After the visitors left, she came and insulted me very well. Since I knew that I had been caught, I pleaded with her to allow me finish my dressing and give her an explanation. She felt that I thought I was above the Kondengui laws, so she continued with her insults and threats of punishment. After dressing, I went to her room to explain what had happened. But she was very angry. According to her, I knew possessing a telephone was illegal and again, I had disobeyed the authorities by refusing to go to the courtyard when asked to go.

This lady had been in and out of prison about three times and she did not want any prisoner changing the status quo the way I was challenging their regulations.

By the time I could talk, this lady jumped up and held me for a fight. I was fed up with their insults. I had a good fight that day. I fought out all the anger and frustrations that were bottled inside me. I had her well beaten up, and because of that, I was disciplined and sanctioned for illegal possession of a telephone and for fighting. I could not leave the female quarters, nor receive my visitors. Friends and relatives came but I could not see them. The warders made my visitors feel very bad, as my name and sanction were posted at the gate of the prison.

After this fight, I gained some respect from those criminals. They realised that I could fight as dirty as they could.

One other thing that marked my early days in Kondengui is this issue of phone possession. On admission into the prison, I had two phones. While searching my things, a chief warder on duty, took away my phones, one very good Nokia phone and a Samsung phone. He told me he was going to hand over the phones the next day when my family came. I had not taken his name and I did not know how to contact him. So I asked my sister who went to enquire from the main office but we could not trace him.

When he heard that my family was looking for him, he came and started negotiating with me that he was going to give me the Nokia phone and keep the Samsung phone for himself.

I asked him why he wanted to keep my phone.

He said he was doing me a favour, because having a phone in prison was illegal. I told him that since it was illegal, I did not want any problem that he should hand over my phones to my relatives. Since I did not agree to do what he wanted, this warder, Mr Medjo, resolved to own my Samsung phone, and to give the Nokia phone to another female prisoner. Both phones had my sim cards in them.

One day I was sleeping and the phone was handed over to me without a sim card and with the memory deleted. When I saw the phone, I sent it out. I didn't want to have problems with these people. I asked to see the medical doctor on grounds of ill health and I narrated the whole episode to him and also asked him to collect my phone from Mr Medjo. He called Mr Medjo and collected the Samsung phone. Mr Medjo was really using the phone because when it was shown to me he had deleted everything and put his own pictures and everything inside.

One night at about 11pm, a search team came from the ministry of justice. I was in bed almost sleeping when I realised that there was a lot of fidgeting in the room. Somebody said the prison superintendent had come in with some people. It meant nothing to me until I heard my name called to come out. When I asked to know the person calling for me at night, they said the director. I asked who the director of the prison was.

This time the superintendent himself came and called for me. He happened to be an Anglophone. He came and got me out of bed. Immediately I went out, I was asked to stand outside and not to go back into my room. I said why? A wardress, a policeman and one director from the ministry were assigned to search my things. They picked my things one after the other. They searched my things as I have never imagined. After searching they found the case of an MTN sim card. This was kept as exhibit against me for the possession of a telephone.

The next day, the gendarmes called me for questioning. On questioning by the gendarmes, I explained to them that the case of an MTN sim card happened to have been in my hand bag since I bought the sim card and I did not know that it was illegal keeping it. She insisted that I should bring the phone, and I told her that the prison administration had confiscated all my phones. This Captain drilled me for one hour. At one point I turned and asked her what the matter was. She told me that someone I called the presidency and the number was traced back to me. I remembered what had happened to my phone. I told her I did not call the presidency. I said I brought my phones when I just came. That Mejdo the chief warder collected my two phones. And that they should ask Mr Medjo who called the presidency using my phone number. When they heard me implicate the chief warder, the case died a natural death.

After ten days of being in prison, some other ladies, at least I want to say people who are educated, came in. These ladies had been imprisoned before, were released and then on appeal of their case, they were again sentenced to serve at least 10 years of imprisonment. They were involved in the famous FEICOM case or what became known as the O'Ndong Ndong case. One of them came into my room. And with her presence, the two of us could reason the same way to change the mentality of the other prisoners in the room.

There was marked improvement in the way things were done in the female quarters. These are ladies who had some good level of education and the financial background to live above the level of the hardened criminals who were incarcerated in quarter 5.

While I was shocked with the behaviour of the other female prisoners, these ladies had foreknowledge of the prison and its workings and therefore could appropriately manage the troublemakers.

Fortunately for us, one year later, the former Minister of Primary Education, Madame Haman, was arrested and brought in. About two months later, the former Secretary of

34

State for Secondary Education, Madame Catherine Essomba was also apprehended and sent to the female quarters, for suspicion of embezzlement of public funds.

Now high powered female prisoners were being sent to a place which had never been prepared to accommodate such levels of persons. Unlike male prisoners who were hosted in at least 12 out of the 13quarters of the prison, Women only occupied one – quarter 5. The female prisoners were all put together, but with the male prisoners, there was some class distinction. The minsters were not living with all the pickpockets, those facing life imprisonment for various crimes and even the sick in the same quarters like their female counterparts.

With the presence of female former members of the government, it dawned on the prison administration that there was a problem. The sanitary situation had improved but was not the best. Water supply was still a problem. Some of these special ladies were no longer young enough to stoop down to use the toilet system. The prison administration also did not have money to solve the situation.

After a lot of interventions by the families of these ladies, they were granted the special treatment. This special treatment was an approval to construct a special toilet for the former ministers. But another problem came up; the problem of space. The only available free space was already very insufficient for the normal capacity of 105 inmates.

One of the toilets out of the existing three was eventually converted to a special toilet for all the inmates who were charged for the embezzlement of public funds. This was done by a concerted effort of the prisoners. Some of the rich prisoners – yes, there are very rich prisoners who have everything but their freedom – kept asking for and obtaining concessions. With their riches, they have made their lives very comfortable inside the prison. They continued putting pressure on the prison administration for better living conditions and this administration finally caved in. This was so often the case that some of them actually ended up having private rooms, to the detriment of the poorer female prisoners.

Out of the 7 rooms to host at least 105 – the number was never below 150 – female prisoners, they actually converted one room to a private room, two rooms to semi private rooms to each host 10 persons. The private room was divided into two to create a single room for the former minister. The comfort extended to installation of air conditioners and whatever modern gadget you can imagine. There is a fundamental truth I came to understand: that a lot of the powers that be in the Biya administration frequent the prison corridors, where many of the prisoners they meet are likely to be their one time colleagues. This is a new breed of prisoners, as no one is immune to these accusations of misappropriation of public funds that have become the order of the day.

With their presence in the same cell room with me, my standards of living changed. Instead of living in a crowded room with thirty people, I moved to a 6 bed, air conditioned room.

The cost of living in prison is very expensive. There is no free service. Warders were like leeches sucking off the resources of the prisoners. Warders would organise and make sure that something illegal comes into the quarters provided the receiving prisoner was ready to pay to get it there. There was always the exchange of money for one service or the other. Anything from the outside world you wanted in prison, you could always get it through a warder. Even guns were smuggled in through the warders. They organised the entry of illegal goods and as far as you continued to pay there was no problem. When you could not pay, they organised searches, and if you were not smart enough to hide the goods, you ended up with a sanction, or if you desperately needed the item you paid more to get it back.

There was an instance where I handed over my phone to a wardress to ensure that a phone was not found on me during a search organised by gendarmes. To retrieve the phone, the lady requested for ten thousand francs. I had to pay and kept paying because she now knew that I had a phone.

You can only appreciate the freedom of movement that you mostly take for granted as a citizen when you are in prison. We needed a written authorisation from the prison administration to move from one section of the prison to the other. Only women and low level or poor prisoners need these authorisations. Interestingly, the prisoners who were sentenced to death and those in shackles were not supposed to move freely but in most cases they seem to have more privileges than the rest of the prison community.

Chapter Five

I did not know that being a client of a lawyer could be so complicated. While still in police custody, I finally had a lawyer who accepted to represent me. Not being comfortable with this lawyer because he was French speaking, I told my husband that I wanted an English speaking lawyer to stand by me and explain the legal language to me, in case I get confused with all their legal jargon. My husband went and paid money to this lawyer Fombad, or whatever they call him.

This boy of a lawyer came to see me at Kondengui one day, left and never ever appeared again. When they called him, he refused to answer. When my husband insisted one day, he asked whether it was by force that he had to represent me and just withdrew from the case. I later heard that he only came to collect his own share of what I had stolen from the government. I had no other option than working with the francophone lawyer.

The very first time I came to face with the examining magistrate again was nine months after I signed the reprimand warrant, although they made me sign a renewal of the reprimand warrant at six months of awaiting trial in prison.

When you are in prison, you learn to play the tricks of prisoners. I had been in prison about six months when one day names were passing from mouth to mouth in the courtyard, of persons who had to go to court that morning. I heard the name of a certain Chia and quickly went and had myself ready. I was fed up of sitting in the same place for months on end. Since many warders did not know me by then, I was escorted to the Court of Appeal. After the roll call the name of the lady I was supposed to be representing was called. Fortunately for me she was not in court. So I quickly told the court registrar and the chief warder that I thought that the name was mine and everybody sympathised with me.

Being my first day in any court of law, and an unconcerned observer, I realised that the job of a magistrate could be very monotonous. After this session, I seized the opportunity and asked one of the warders who had escorted me to take me to see the new permanent secretary of the national committee to fight HIV/AIDS. I had some issues to sort out with him like payment of my allowances and making available the justification documents which I needed for my defence.

You will not believe the surprise that was on the faces of the persons we met. They thought I had gone through the door of no return like what happened during the slave trade. Whatever I requested for on that day he promised, just to make sure that I left his office. Needless to say that he did nothing to assist me or pay my dues after that encounter.

Back to my session with the examining magistrate on the first day, who confessed to me that the case was too technical, and for that reason he would want me to explain to him how the project was managed at the provincial level, adding that he already had a picture of how it was managed at the national level. All he knew was that we were accused of misappropriation of public funds.

I spent six days explaining the functioning of the provincial technical group for the fight against HIV/AIDS and the roles and functions of all the staff. On the eighth day, I was questioned on the charges against me. This took two days. He wanted to know why I did not provide the justification documents. Did I really spend this money? He insisted I should make the documents available.

When I came out, I was expecting my lawyer to encourage me, to tell me, 'Madame, you have done well.'

But the lawyer turned around and asked me, 'Does your husband know that he has not completed my money?' I was so shocked that I burst out into tears. I thought I was dealing with a human being who felt for me. Maybe it was part of the trade not to empathise with the client. I told him that was the last thing I expected him to say at such a momentous juncture. I needed a word of encouragement from him or criticism on how I answered the questions and not a story about money.

He told me his father was not well and that he needed the money. There and then, fortunately, my sister was there. I took her phone and called my husband. I said the lawyer wants his money. He said, 'I have already given that man two thirds of his money.' The lawyer had agreed on three million. They gave him two million and still he wanted all his money, even before the case in court had come to a head. Anyway, my husband subsequently paid all the money to the lawyer.

Since our responses seemed to show that there was no misappropriation of funds and also due to the fact that the programmes we were managing followed the guiding principles of the funders, the examining magistrate and the state's counsel, hired expert controllers, another independent organisation to carry out a counter control in the field. Their control concluded that it was impossible for me to embezzle that money. Given all the checks and balances that were in place, it was not possible for me to have embezzled that money. But that notwithstanding, the examining magistrate still sent the case in front of the open court sixteen months after declaring that they wanted the justification documents.

For the counter control to take place, the controllers needed the former accountant Mr Nguimpack, whom they contacted. The former accountant showed them where all the justification documents were kept. So they collected a good number of the justification documents and they brought them back to Yaoundé. And that is what even assisted me to defend my case. Because when they came, I don't know what happened at the level of the court, the court could not also handle all the documents. They took the documents and they mixed them up. But fortunately, they gave me copies of what they brought. So when the examining magistrate was forwarding the case in front of the court, he presented the few justification documents that he could lay hands on. Later we learnt that instructions came from higher quarters that anybody who was controlling money should go and answer in front of the court. That was one of the main reasons why I was sent to go and answer in front of the court. Had it just been on the basis of the experts' report and my defence, I think the examining magistrate would have let me go after eighteen months in detention.

Something interesting happened on the day they called for us to send us in front of the court, when we went to take the final report of the examining magistrate. I called for my lawyer and told him I had been subpoenaed to the office of the examining magistrate, expecting to see him on arrival. He did not show up and up till date he has never asked me or told me what happened. After all, he already had all his money.

I needed a lawyer. And so comes in the third lawyer. I was now going in front of the bar with nobody to defend me and they were telling me if you don't have a lawyer, the government was going to assign you a lawyer. And in such a situation when the government assigns a lawyer, the lawyer will only be interested in getting his money from the government and not interested in defending me. So when they said that, I refused to be assigned to a lawyer by the government.

I got the new lawyer through the intervention of an in-law and after they saw the counter control report. This new lawyer is quite interesting. He knew his job but was very busy with other big name clients, the bar council and politics. He asked me to write down my own defence simulating all the possible questions I thought I could be asked. And that is what I did, I wrote my own defence and I gave him.

One of the things I asked him was to ask for a disjoinder from the case concerning Olangena Awono Urbain and others. I wanted a hearing of my own case, since according to the report, the misdemeanour took place in the South west Province of Cameroon. Therefore, the Court of Mfoundi did not have any jurisdiction to hear my case.

My lawyer, thinking that he was doing something good, left, went and told Olangena that that was what I was planning to do.

My God!! The next two hours, Olangena came looking for me furiously. What do I want? I am going to drag the case down.

I said yes. In the first place, they are accusing me of something that took place in the South-West province and they are saying Olangena and others. How could that be? I asked him, 'Do you know what I was managing in the South-West?' I said, 'You have your own case, I have my own. Why should I be under you?' And for one reason or the other, I told him, 'I even heard that they sent me in front of the bar because of you, because they believed that all of us managers, embezzled.' I said, 'Please, I want to go back to the South-West where I am going to meet magistrates who even understand the same language, and I will have witnesses to stand up for me.' Bringing witnesses to Yaounde meant paying their transport and lodging. My family did not have that type of money.

The man was very furious that I was going to delay the case before the hearing could even start. The lawyer apologised, saying he did not know that applying for a disjoinder was going to bring a problem. So he said that he was going to withdraw the application for the disjoinder.

And with that, the hearing of the case started. As it turned out, Mr Olangena ended up delaying the case because one aspect of his case was taken to the Appeal Court, then to the Supreme Court. We wasted one year waiting for the final decision from one appeal court to the other.

It didn't help matters that there was so much animosity between Olangena and the prosecuting authority. They were just very rude to each other. There was a lot of suspicion and fear on both sides that one day in court, a lawyer informed us that a dead cat was found at the door of the president's office. It seemed as if they knew themselves under different circumstances because at one point we were informed that this president wanted to be taken off the case. At one point Mr Olangena turned around again and applied for a change of presiding magistrate because of conflict of interest and incompatibility.

For this reason, we wasted six months again waiting for a change of the president of the court, which meant that the whole panel of judges was going to be changed.

The new judge started very well. Along the line, he was again taken off the case and another lady judge came in as presiding magistrate. This time we were told that he was called to other duties but the real reason is that he was very impartial and would not give in to the threats of the state's counsel. The court hearing was progressing smoothly even under this new presiding judge and she promised that she was willing to complete the case within one year. That was our fourth year in prison awaiting trial.

The court sessions were very interesting because I saw the determination of the state and the controllers to accuse us and with the combined efforts of our lawyers we were bent on overturning the charges against us. The controllers were represented by the head of mission Mr Bayoi

During one of the sessions of cross examination of the witnesses for the state, I accused Mr Bayoi of coming with preconceived ideas concerning me during his control mission. I asked him why in their report they did not so much as make any allusion to the fact that they saw the accountant and worked with him. At this point in time I had learnt that he and the accountant came from the same village, and I wanted to draw the attention of the court to the fact that that was one of the main reasons why the accountant was free and I was in prison in his place. If it is true that there was embezzlement, is it possible for me to have embezzled alone? The accountant was in charge of finances. Is it possible that I should embezzle and the accountant will never even made any report? He was the one who had to initiate any financial transaction. And if he did not visa it, I did not sign. So how did it happen that I was being accused alone to have embezzled? Why was I standing in court alone?

I reminded Mr Bayoi that when he was doing his control, he was doing it in Bassa, because that accountant was a Bassa boy. It was not in French or English, the official languages of the Cameroon public service.

Mr Bayoi downplayed the implication of what I was saying. He insisted he had nothing personal against me. He further explained that, before they go to the field, they have to do a lot of background work, get a lot of information. He said when they came for control in Buea, they had a lot of information concerning me. And their role was to confirm or disapprove the information.

Interestingly, Mr Bayoi started his career at the state control under the tutelage of Mr Olangena and for this reason, the former Minister could not stomach the fact somebody who could not write a good report when they were working together could be the one writing and accusing him of misappropriation of funds. You can imagine how tense the cross examination sessions between Mr Olangena and Mr Bayoi were. At times both of them had to be called to order by the judge. Because Bayoi thought there was a threat against his life, there were instances he came to court accompanied by policemen

Fortunately or unfortunately, Mr Bayoi went on retirement at the end of that year and was replaced by another team member.

In the fourth year we were hoping that the case would come to an end either positively or negatively as far as instructions were given to the judges to decide. We had been informed that the hearings were just window dressings, and that the outcome of all the 'Epervier' – as the arrests were conducted under 'operation Epervier' in French or 'Operation Sparrow Hawk' – cases had already been decided even before the arrests.

In the first week of October 2012, our lawyers had all presented their summaries and pleaded with judges for leniency. The court hall was jammed full with spectators, family members and lawyers. All of them brilliantly presented their summations. It was a teaching session for junior lawyers, because our type of case was a first and there were foreign lawyers defending Mr Olangena.

On 12 of October 2012, we were told it was the D day for judgment to be passed. On this particular day, we knew we were expected in court so we got ready as early as 8 am and we waited to be taken to court. Until mid-day no one came for us, our family members were sitting in court waiting for us and the magistrates to show up. The lawyers did not have any information to give our family members.

About five pm that evening, the lawyers met one state council in town and he said nobody should quote him. They had been given instructions that none of them should appear in court on that day. So around nine o'clock, the presiding judge, finally went and declared that because the state council had not come, she could not read the judgment. She further went ahead and adjoined the case to the special criminal court that had just been created and gone functional on the 13th of October 2012.

At the special criminal court, we started all over again in December 2012. It was the same procedure with the same witnesses but the only difference was we were in a new court meeting a new set of legal minds who had been specially selected and appointed to try special criminal matters, especially embezzlement of public funds.

The best thing that happened to me is that Mr Bayoi retired and was replaced by an overzealous colleague called Mpouli-Mpouli, whom I believed had not yet developed good skills to lie with the impunity of Mr Bayoi. The other members of the team never showed up in court again. Since Mr Mpouli Mpouli could not stand up to the battery of questions from my lawyer, he ended on cross examination by telling everyone in court that the control team was following instructions and they only wrote down what they were instructed to write.

From the day he made that admission in court, I had renewed confidence that whatever happened, I was going to be freed. My lawyer was going to build his final arguments around that admission.

The hearing was very fast and exactly 9 months after the hearing started, judgement was passed.

I was discharged and acquitted after being declared not guilty for all the accusation counts against me.

Chapter Six

W hen I tell people today that God wanted me to go to that prison for a reason, I mean it.

In prison, I learnt to completely depend on Him.

Before going to prison, I thought I was a believer, but I think I truly became one in prison.

If you are in prison and you don't take time off to pray, you will either become a hardened criminal or you will be so filled with hatred that on your release you can end up a killer, because of lack of forgiveness.

Inside the prison, I was taught how to forgive, to let go a lot of things. I was taught to see others just as instruments and tools in the hand of God or the devil depending on the roles they played to influence your destiny.

We had workshops and seminars led by men of God. What struck me most was this particular workshop organised by a French Canadian evangelist Mr Marc André on Christian life. This took place the very first year I went to prison. It was a 5 day workshop and we were given one whole day to think over and write down a list of persons we had hurt and another of those who had hurt us. We were asked to write letters to these persons and actually tell them that we had forgiven them.

It is big therapy. When I called and told friends and family members with whom I was having issues that I was wrong and asking for forgiveness, it felt as if I had abscesses that were being drained.

I even searched for a means of getting into contact with Mr Nguimpack, my former accountant. But unfortunately, he refused to have anything to do with me. During my defence in court, I wanted him to stand as my witness, but he refused to come. I sent my lawyer and my brother to convince him, but immediately he saw a word from them, he disappeared. At one point they even gave me his number. I sent a message telling him that he should not be afraid. I did not want to hurt him. I just wanted him to come and let us make peace. Up till date, he has never ever replied to that message.

I learnt how to live with the lowest of the people and with the biggest. I met people of all walks of life in prison.

The very first time I saw overt lesbians and homosexuals was in prison. I did not know that they existed in Cameroon.

They were those who came to prison because of their lesbian way of life outside the prison and those who got initiated into the gay way of life in prison. Take for instance, someone like Joey, the boy-girl I talked about earlier. She is a lesbian. The presence of Joey excited many young girls, mostly those who lived free lives outside the prison. The craving for sex made them to give in to those types of things. There was the case of two homosexual boys who were arrested and brought in because they were caught 'en flagrant délit' as the French will say. These boys almost caused a sex riot in the male quarters. In fact, the prison administration did not know what to do with them. They moved them constantly from one male quarter to another. The problem posed by locking men up for long periods away from any contact with the opposite sex, was real. The same was true of females. It's that craving for sex and all that. It's not as if the people have that lesbian tendency or the homosexual tendency. It is because they have been locked up and their needs are dire.

Sharing the same intimate environment in close proximity only made matters worse. You are always around each other; you are bathing together and yearning for sex together. At one point it became an epidemic among the young girls in the female quarter. The lack of accommodation meant that twelve year old girls were locked up in the same place with twenty year olds and that is how they got initiated into all types of deviant behaviour.

There are men who no longer know how to live in freedom. They have been in and out so many times that the only place where they are truly comfortable is in prison.

In prison, you don't see the real hardened criminals mixing up with others. During the day, they stay in their rooms and only leave in the evening to stroll around the courtyard. While in prison, they still have their gang members outside and they coordinate them from inside the prison cells. They are in their beds coordinating activities outside, giving instructions to their gang members outside, telling them what to do. When you come across one of them and they happen to tell you things that they do, these are horrible things. They are well connected to the big people out there. Their physical absence from the wider society must not blind us to their active presence through the network of gangsters that do their bidding.

The machinery they have put in place is so good, so much so that they succeeded in collecting money from two senate aspirants. I don't know how they got wind of the fact that these people wanted to be senators at all cost. So, they contacted them and told them that they were the middle men collecting money for the president of the republic. Just before the final list of the senators was released, these guys sent their outside contact to hire a room at the Hilton Hotel and then make sure that these would be senators came and paid the money to him. The men each paid thirty million francs. The money was then split among themselves with the warders having their own share. Interestingly enough, one of the persons from whom they collected the thirty million succeeded to become a senator.

There were stories about wives who came to visit their husbands in the prison and ended up being duped by other male prisoners.

There is a common situation where girls receive calls from unknown persons in prison, asking these girls to bring them food and many other items from town. Before they come, these prisoners would arrange with warders to ensure that they come in hitch free, and while inside, they discover that these so called very important personalities were just prisoners. Some of these ladies came and continued coming depending on the degree of lies they were fed.

There was this very interesting situation where friends in crime met in the female quarters but for different charges. These ladies connived with a lady working for one of the local banks. Since the bank worker was greedy and wanted to grow rich very fast, three other ladies lured her to collect 25 million from the bank and give them to go and multiply the way money-doublers are known to do.

In the group was a very fat girl from Pinyin. She played the part of the sorcerer. They showed this lady where she was going to bring the money, an uncompleted building. This lady then took the money for multiplication. Immediately the fat sorcerer collected the 25 million, the others frightened the bank worker and asked her to come back after two hours. On coming back they had disappeared.

She was arrested and sent to prison after she was controlled and found to be short by 25 million. While in prison, the gang of three that deceived her came in for other charges not connected to her. They pretended not know each other but in the dark they spent their time quarrelling.

One day, I was sitting with the fat lady called Ajara, and I asked her whether she knew the lady from the bank whose name is Agripine. She told me that they dealt with her because she was very greedy. I asked her why she considered the lady greedy instead of being remorseful for what they did to her. She told me that she could not regret the act because this lady in particular was very gullible. According to Ajara, they did not steal from the bank. Agripine brought the money out of her own free will. She did not want to get involved in invoking the devil but she wanted the devil's money. Ajara and her accomplices played a trick on Agripine and took away all the money and went and bought land and cars.

Ajara gave me this advice because she did not want me to be one day deceived. She advised me to be very careful in particular in taxis. She and other fraudsters like her mostly operate inside taxis. She told me they are usually well dressed and always moving as gangs of at least 3 to 4 persons. Immediately they discover that you have some money, one of them will start a general conversation concerning big money and businesses. If you become interested and contribute to their conversation, you have already fallen prey to them. After that, it seems as if you were hypnotised to give everything you have in order to receive more. She asked me to go and ask Agripine whether she knew her. One day I asked Agripine, whether she knew Ajara before coming to prison. Agripine said yes, 'I know her, and I am waiting for her outside the walls of the prison to settle the matter.'

The interesting thing is that the bank finally lost its money. Agripine's relatives raised some money which she paid to her judge and the case was dismissed. At the end of the day, I wonder whether it is even worth the pain locking up people after everything when you know how corrupt the judiciary is in this country. It is a well-known fact that only the poor in this country go to prison and stay in prison.

The appearance of rich people in prison is a very recent thing. It is only the operation Epervier that opened the doors of the prison to the group of Cameroonians that we normally regard as rich and elite such as former ministers, directors of state corporations and prime ministers.

In Kondengui, these former ministers are lodged in special quarters. There are three of such special quarters. With the coming of the prime minister, a new building was raised to accommodate him. They cannot live all their lives locked up in their rooms, so once in a while they mix up with the lower down prisoners in the court yards and in church. Having special quarters was normal for men, but not for women. It was not that common to have women of a certain class in prison.

Those who built our prisons did not foresee that women of status would one day be sent the way of their prisons. Until recently, the practice had just been to put everybody together, which has been the cry of all the female prisoners. I don't blame the prison administration, because they never thought that women of a certain level could go to prison.

In the society, it has never been easy to have women living together and it was the same situation with the high society women in prison. Two big society women were put in the same room and their fights and quarrels became legendary. I've never seen that type of fighting or heard those type of insults before. I think some of their fights were even published in the newspapers. I don't know how the newspapers got wind of their quarrels and fights. The cause of these fights was just competition, a lot of jealousy, and one person trying to show that they are more financially viable than the other.

Some high profile criminals are not brought to Kondengui because the state would like to monitor and control them better. They are incarcerated at the Gendarmerie, where the state can have a special eye on them. It's more open there though, with family and friends allowed to visit, and bring you amenities. Prisoners are allowed access to computers and to the internet and all that. They are guarded by Gendarmes who do not live the beggarly life that warders live.

Famous people who come to Kondengui become very famous with the prisoners. The ordinary prisoners start crowding around them, currying favours. Take somebody like Mr Michel Fotso. When he was brought in, he wanted to change the face of Kondengui. At least the poor and young prisoners received assistance from him. There were cases like those prisoners who had been judged and who could not leave because they could not pay their court fines. Mr Fotso, through his lawyers, paid these court fines. Every week, I think it was every week, he organised a meal from Hilton Hotel to feed the young prisoners. It was like Father Christmas had come to Kondengui. He assisted a lot of prisoners who had financial problems. I can remember that during the women's day celebration of 2011 he provided a meal and supplied all the women with the 8th March wrappers. He was becoming very popular, and with this popularity he could recruit just anybody to do anything for him.

Mr Marafa, on the contrary, was very famous outside the prison and he even had sympathisers who followed him to prison. At least, I know of five persons who caused disorder and were sent to prison because of Marapha. The Fotso and Marafa duo was too much and had to be isolated.

Former Prime Minister Ephraim Inoni joined us in Kondengui. The man seems so withdrawn. He does not mix with a lot of people. He leaves from his room down to where he receives visitors and back. He does not mix even with the other ministers. Originally when he just came, some of the ministers used to come and sit with him, but at the end of the day, I realised that he was more reserved. He stopped mixing up with them. And that was before they even passed judgement on him. So maybe he was hoping that being reserved and not mixing with those other ministers that maybe they were going to be more lenient on him, or maybe even set him free. Instead, they gave him twenty five years.

Even less prominent prisoners like us medical doctors would have contributed our modest best had we been allowed. There were five of us, medical doctors in prison, but we did not practice medicine, as much as we would have loved to help out. Originally, a lot of prisoners started coming with their different ailments once they knew that we were medical doctors. The members of the health unit held a meeting and decided that as long as we are awaiting trial, we were not medical doctors. The prison has an infirmary with a doctor and nurses. The place is understaffed with four beds for a population of at least four thousand people. They were a lot of gunshot wounds and many fractures, but the infirmary was not equipped to handle all these cases. Thank God for the presence of a catholic group that trained prisoners to clean some of the wounds and they even ran a dispensary of essential drugs.

The death rate was very high. When I went there, every day a prisoner died. They did not want our help but preferred to use people who knew nothing about medicine. I remember an instance where one boy had a serious problem and one of my colleagues discovered that nothing was done and the boy was dying. One of my medical colleagues ordered treatment. My God! The next day they called for him and ordered him not to come to the infirmary again. He was told to remember that he may have been a medical doctor outside, but not in prison. This was happening even as the doctor of the prison infirmary himself was not available. This was a nurse who ordered a medical doctor to stop treating suffering persons.

The police do not care. They drag the prison criminals with gunshot wounds. I don't blame the police. Somebody went to court with one leg. He was walking about with a crutch, yet he ran away. The warder thought that this man could not run away, so he was not too careful around him. But the next thing, people saw the man running and he outran the warder. So I don't blame the police when they carry criminals with gunshot wounds and come and throw them in prison. Given the low level of care in prison, a great majority of these wounds became gangrenous and even led to leg amputation.

I respected a particular lady till date.She was in prison because she duped a Frenchman living in France while she was here living with the husband who happened to be a pastor. As the story goes, she got connected to this man through the internet and even got married to him. After their marriage, she came back to Cameroon claiming to be pregnant for him. After one year she presented the picture of a baby to this French husband. Overjoyed, he sent money to her to build a clinic and a home, since he was planning to retire in Yaoundé. On being informed that this lady was married he paid a surprised visit to the lady and family just to discover the whole truth and how he had been duped.

Even in prison she came with a big abdomen and informed the prison administration that she was 7 months pregnant and needed special attention. One Sunday night the nurse on duty asked me to attend to her because she had been running a very high fever which was not responding to any drug. When I went to her bed, she refused to move. I realised that she was lying on one side under thick blankets. Immediately I removed the bed covers, the temperature on the exposed side dropped. The temperature was 36.5 degrees Celsius, but the side on which she was lying was burning at 42 degrees. Then I realised that she was lying on a hot water bottle and will not let go of it. When I insisted that she let go of the water bottle she became delirious and declared that she did not want to see me. I had to write down my findings, including the fact that she was not pregnant. Since I had discovered her trick, we became enemies. She had to stage this act, because, with the pregnancy, she could be escorted to the hospital in town as an emergency, without waiting for the approval of the courts.

I think I was more informed when I was in prison concerning Cameroon in general, and the government in particular, than now that I am outside. In prison, we knew everything happening outside, especially in government circles. The fact that Kondengui has prisoners from all walks of life, and that these prisoners still have family members and friends outside, accounts in part for our ease of access to information about the world outside. Many a prisoner has friends in privileged places, including in government. So, all information that is available out there is accessible from in here. The fact that cell phones are available collapses the Chinese wall between prison and the outside.

A good case in point is this. Before Prime Minister Ephraim Inoni was brought in, we knew already that something was going to happen. Not only because someone was contracted to put up a storey building in six months, but also because as the building was being erected, some very connected prisoners kept saying that the building was for Prime Minister Inoni. This was well before he was arrested. Prisoners are really informed. Soon after the building was completed, Inoni was brought in. Both Inoni and Fotso were arrested at the same time. Inoni was given the whole of the new building to himself. They made him comfortable. He slept upstairs and received visitors downstairs. He was not receiving in the open like every other person. He had a sitting room where people came to see him. And he even had two warders assigned to him alone. His wife had the permission to come and go. They gave him preferential treatment and he was closest to the female quarters. I saw him every day of the rest of my stay in that place.

Chapter Seven

In Kondengui the social activities and your own commitment to these social activities evolve as the years go by. I have already mentioned briefly the reception committee that received us when we arrived there the first time. This reception is reserved for everybody who comes in. It's like they want to instil the fear of the prison in you.

Immediately you come in, there is that reception committee. They make a lot of noise. There is a lot of booing and jeering. And the next thing they tell you is they are going to bring you cockroach soya or cockroach stew.

When they instil that fear in you, even if you are as hard-hearted as what, you get frightened.

That's what happened during the very first two years when I went there. You had these groups of women that would come in and are immediately warned.

When the warders open the gates, you have this impression that you are entering a hole. They push you inside, and as soon as you are in, you meet a crowd of faces waiting to receive you. Then the next thing you hear is the booing and jeering. And you hear 'asoya, asoya, asoya'. It's a word in Ewondo meaning, 'welcome, there is a newcomer, welcome.' And when one person says 'asoya', everybody comes out to see the new arrival.

If you are young, the young girls start warning you off their boyfriends in the male quarters. You are told not to dare talk to the boyfriends if you value your life. They just start telling you everything about themselves, and warning you against what you are not supposed to do in prison. Everybody is threatened by a new face. For one thing, the new person coming in is seen as still financially viable. It means you are still

61

bringing some good stuff. You are a new face in the complex and it means the male prisoners will be interested in you.

In case you are an elderly woman coming in, they don't care about you. They want to make noise. As you're coming here know that you are a mother outside, you are not a mother inside. I left my mother outside so don't carry your maternal airs from outside here and bring them inside here.

Young or old, everybody will want to hear your story. If you're not careful, when you open your mouth and you tell them your story, know that the next day they are going to use that story to insult you. When you come, they are pulling you, seeking to know what happened. Where were you? What did you do? If you are foolish enough to talk, thinking that they are sympathising with you, you are at their mercy. Your story gives them the power to make your life hell.

One will tell you, 'You see, I have been here for six years, this is what I did...' When you hear such a story, you open up and you start telling them your story. Because you are still very naïve, you don't yet know the prison, you don't yet know the dynamics, you open your mouth and you tell them. The next thing is that they will use it against you.

The government has informants and they know that it's only when you are so vulnerable that you can tell the truth. So the informants come around you and you tell them the real story and that is how your story goes back to the court. That is what usually happens when a new inmate is admitted in the female quarters. I cannot talk too much about the male quarters because I don't really know what happened there.

The female quarter is the fifth quarter out of thirteen quarters in Kondengui prison. Originally, the female quarter was meant to have an enrolment of 85 prisoners, fifteen per room. But eventually, the number of female inmates became more than the capacity that that quarter could take. We thought that it was an arrangement at the courts, to ensure that the prisons were overcrowded, by judging very few cases at a time. Every now and then a census was conducted to find out prisoners who spent a long time awaiting trial, but even with that exercise, the situation did not change.

It was during such census that they discovered some prisoners who had stayed in prison for over five years without trial and not even having files in the prison. Most of these censuses took place after many human right groups mounted pressure on the government in protest of the deplorable situation in which the prisoners were kept.

The social dynamics inside the prison is just the same like we find outside. You find the same suspicions, intrigues and jealousy. You easily hear comments like, 'I have spent so many years in prison and you should also spend the same time.' Prison is a microcosm of the society outside. If Cameroon is Africa in miniature as we love to claim, prison is Cameroon in miniature.

Life within was more interesting on the days of court hearings. The person going to court had to keep it top secret for fear that other inmates can hear about it and perform some type of magic, which will lead to their condemnation or their being sentenced severely or their cases being adjourned.

A lot of people are in prison for witchcraft, and people fear witchcraft. There was one lady who came and she spent all her time in the toilet. Every hour you went in she was doing one thing or the other in the toilet. One day, she was brought out in front of everybody and warned not to try any of her witchcraft in prison, for bigger witches will bring her down. But that does not stop the fact that people still sleep at night and say, 'I slept at night and this person came and was disturbing me.' Or 'You are the person who is blocking me from leaving the prison.' And 'My case is not moving on, because so and so person is making witchcraft for me not to go.' So people generally kept it to themselves when a hearing was scheduled.

The only way we suspected that somebody was going to go to court was when they intensified their spiritual activities. When they prayed more and became more reserved. Otherwise, they will not say anything. There was this rumour around that when you tell people they will go and block you. For the really superstitious people, when they went to court and were released or maybe finished serving time, they did not tell anybody, and we only noticed that they were packing their things and sending home under the pretext that they wanted a change of clothes.

In most instances, when a lady was released at court, immediately she crosses the gate into the quarter, she erupts into singing and dancing. Then, a crowd quickly gathered around her and that is how the quarters became alive with singing, dancing and jubilation.

During such occasions, almost everyone came to share in your joy and victory.

In my own case, the dancing and jubilation took two days. It was the first time in the special criminal court that a prison inmate was declared not guilty. This made others who were awaiting trial like me to have hopes of also being released.

Before this time, all those who were arrested under 'operation Epervier' knew that the least number of years anyone could be sentenced is 10 years and we already had many cases doing time. While I was waiting for the judges and the state council to do the final formalities before releasing me, I spent time encouraging others.

You will think that immediately you are discharged and acquitted in court that you are free to leave prison immediately, but, unfortunately, it is not the case. Even if all the warders are present when the declaration is made in court, until the release documents are received in prison you are still a prisoner.

I witnessed a case where a man was discharged and acquitted in court and stayed in prison for over six months waiting for the release documents to be sent to the prison. What happened in this situation was that the magistrate, after passing judgement, was transferred and therefore did not write down the judgement before leaving for transfer. This man had to be tried again by another judge after serious negotiations by the family.

Incompetence and indifference are a nightmare in the broad daylight of the Cameroonian judiciary.

A normal day in prison started with singing as early as 4 a.m. It was the first thing that woke me up the first day I arrived in Kondengui, apart from the rats, that is. God, I went to bed at 2:30 and I barely slept for thirty minutes and the next thing I heard was singing. Little did I know that singing was going to become a way of life for my almost six years as an inmate.

This is what still happens today. The Pentecostal group starts singing at 4am. They have one hour of prayer. From 5 o'clock to 6 am the Catholics take over. Then the Protestants come in from 5:30 to 6:30. That is on a normal very beautiful day.

You are fortunate that that's the only thing that wakes you up, that beautiful singing, praise and worship unto the lord. And if you belong to any of these groups, you just get up and go and join them.

It's only in prison that I saw how religious we can be. You see religious fights. People insult each other and even fight over it. You see each person hanging on their religion. It's only in prison that I saw that. It exists out there in the greater society, but not to that extent. And we had all types of religious organisations in that place, even Muslims, had their own prayers. We guarded our prayer spaces religiously. This space is a shade about 10 metres long and 4 metres wide, divided into portions for the different religious groups. Since the same space was also used for recreation, we also sat down according to our religious affiliations. The prisoners made benches which they used for all these activities and when prayers are over, the benches are used to guard the space so that nobody comes and desecrates prayer grounds.

Another thing that struck me that first night of my imprisonment was the display of jerry cans, piles and piles of jerry cans of different colours and sizes on the courtyard. The commandant of the quarter, among the many words of advice she gave me was to ask my family to bring me two jerry cans because of water problems.

I was admitted into a place where we were permitted to use only plastic containers. The only metal cutlery I was permitted to own was spoons. Otherwise plates, cups and knives were plastic. Although as time went by, I exchanged these plastics for breakable plates and cups and ended up even having knives and forks in metal. This only took place when I had been in prison for over six months and could now negotiate with the warders who, with money, could make the impossible possible.

While prayers are still going on, someone will start shouting 'la court!' Another is shouting 'Douche!', and then you hear another 'Braunderie'. This is for the persons who are supposed to clean this places to start work, because if they waited for daylight, there will be no space for cleaning to be done. In the different rooms cleaning started as early as 4 am. Since the floors were rough, they cleaned with very hard brushes. When they were cleaning rooms, all those who were sleeping on floors had to carry their mattresses out to the courtyard. It was a pathetic sight during the rainy season. Most of these activities ended up with fights because of the overcrowding. You don't need anything to start the fight. And when I say fight it is real fighting, involving the flying lids of pots, and even the flashing of knives.

This was a common occurrence and two days could not pass by without you having such a scenario. As part of the sanctions the persons fighting were chained together by chaining the arm of one to the leg of the other person. Otherwise, they will chain both your arms or your legs to the arms or legs of the person you were fighting with. And you will stay like that depending on the temperament of the warder in charge. He can keep you there for 24 hours, 48 hours even. If one of them wanted to visit the toilet both of them had to go. There was no choice. You had to carry the burden of your provocation along.

Another exciting event was visiting days. This took place on Sundays, Tuesdays, and Thursdays, and on public holidays as from 10 am to 4 pm. These days always reminded me of boarding school. The expectation of seeing someone from home, bringing you food and money, was a tonic that brought us new energy and hope. You can imagine the disappointment or feelings of those who did not have any visitors.

There were two types of visitors: those from town and those from within the prison. I mean other inmates. There was this scenario where the male inmates had girlfriends in the female quarters. I don't mean that they came in as couples. These are relationships that naturally developed inside the prison. They were some males who spent their time scouting for new female inmates. During registration they lingered around the warders just to get the names of these ladies. The next thing was the lady received a letter from some male with a lot of lies and requesting for their friendship. The gullible females fell for it and that is how many of the relationships developed. In the course of an imprisonment you could find a lady changing as many as three to five male friends, depending on how comfortable they were in the relationships. These relationships were encouraged and pursued under the watchful eyes of the prison administration.

There were too many gossips chasing our credulity about some of these relationships. When you find yourself inside such a place, what do you really expect? We had this particular girl. She was a very pretty girl, one of the movers and shakers in prison, just as she was in the outside world. You find two male inmates fighting over this girl. And the next thing is to prove that that girl is not as good as the other girls. Somebody came with the story that she is homosexual. This story moved around the place like wildfire. The story was circulated by another girl, a rival, who was interested in one of the men fighting over her. It's not only rumour and gossip that are commonplace in prison relationships; poison moves around as well, and several lovers have lost their lives to the jealousy of poison.

When the going was good, what happened in these relationships was, the girlfriends prepared food for the boyfriends who were called 'RADAR'. The food was sent to the males through messenger services. These were the poorer prisoners who were called 'TAXI'. These human taxis were the most expensive and you paid them in cash or in kind. After the Radar had his meal, he came visiting the female quarters as from 5 pm. The female quarters was called the 'NGASSE', which means trap in Ewondo. The men paid as much as 1000 FCFA for these visits. Whatever transpired outside during this period, God alone knows. These were strictly paid visits for a few. After these visits the radar left money for breakfast to be delivered to him by the taxi.

It was an interesting sight. Around 4pm the females prepared themselves, wore very beautiful dresses, and then with a beautifully presented tray of food, went out.

The visiting spot was a corridor which was used for a sacristy by the Catholics. These visits took place under the watchful eyes of the warders who sat and pretended that they were not seeing what the couples were doing. It was a privilege to be a warder sitting in front of the female quarters, because there you have many more tips than any of your counterparts working elsewhere in the prison.

Even our visitors from outside had to tip the warders. They had put a system in place where you paid a certain amount before you could be allowed into the corridor of the female quarters. To use the bench the visitor also had to pay. Otherwise you would have sat at the general courtyard where everybody sat with all the pickpockets who harassed you for money. For a bit of comfort, or visitors paid the warders to sit at the corridor of the female quarters and to sit on the bench.

Even when you are going with your visitor's card you also pay somebody at the gate. Things were made possible through money changing hands.

Mme Haman had an open authorisation for all her visitors, and this authorisation permitted her visitors to spend the whole day in prison. The chief warder, Mr Aloua, recognised manna when it fell from heaven. Just from the visitors of Mrs Haman, he could make all the money that he needed for one month. Due to this, he restricted the visiting hours of the radars. There were instances when he collected money but refused that they spend time with the ladies. Fortunately for the radars, Mr Aloua went on retirement and was replaced by another who reinstated the former system.

The intrigues among the warders were phenomenal. I was privileged to have an English speaking wardress working at the female quarters by name Therese. Her colleagues did not understand how she, being an Anglophone, could be posted to the coveted post of sitting in front of the female quarters. There was open hostility towards her and in some cases they used inmates to insult her. She is quite knowledgeable for level of education and could communicate with anyone without a complex. Given her openness, almost all the former ministers used her as a pretext to visit the female quarters.

After some time, I realised that she was not the attraction but that she was a discreet means for them relating with the female inmates. One minister even started dating a girl and they used her as a screen to curious eyes. This continued until her colleagues got wind of the situation and set her up. One evening somebody just came and informed me that my sister had been asked to pack her things and go, to leave the quarters. Later, she told me that it was alleged that she arranged for the minster and the girls to have sex in the chaplain's office. It was a shock to me to imagine that people could stoop so low in order to make others pay. To show how bent the colleagues had decided to destroy her career, they even claimed that she became pregnant for an inmate. This inmate happened to be my colleague who became friendly with her because of me. A wardress even took the story to my colleague's wife who met Therese and showered her with insults.

When one is deprived of their freedom the way it was taken away from us, one devises strategies to get some freedom or go to the outside world even if it is just for a few hours.

In the early days of our imprisonment, when we were authorized to go to the hospital we were assigned one or two warders as escorts. You could choose the warders to escort you depending on how much money you gave to the prison administration. Many at times the warders signed you out and you went your separate ways in front of the prison gates. The amount paid ranged from 5000 FCFA to 10,000 FCFA a day per warder. To be on the safe side we went to the hospital, had our consultations and went home, for those who had homes in Yaoundé.

We continued enjoying this home going until the gendarmerie got wind of it. The former Minister of Finance Mr Abah Abah was authorised to go to the hospital, which he did and he was escorted by four warders. On arrival, his consulting doctor was in the theatre, so he and his escorts went to his house. Little did they know that the Secretary of State for Defence who happened to be his neighbour had been tipped off. Immediately the prison bus drove into his compound, the next thing he saw was the mobile intervention unit behind him, who surrendered him and his escorts and carried them to the gendarmerie. He and his warders are serving time for attempted prison break.

Take for instance, what happened with one of the persons in my case, Yves Mbella Rodrigue. He used the hospital as a means to run away from prison and to leave this country. What happened was that Mbella obtained permission to go to the hospital. He had a health problem that warranted that he go to the hospital monthly for follow-up.

On this particular day, he took these two warders out and gave his car, his Rav4 and asked the warders to go and do whatever they wanted to do, they should take care of their family. I hear he gave them 50,000FCFA each, that they should take care of their family. They should not care about him. They should only come and check for him at his mother-in-law's place. Around 7 o'clock, the prison administration realised that the person who went to the hospital was not yet back, so they were calling to find out whether they had admitted him in the hospital. And when they called the two warders, none of them were answering their phones. When the warders eventually answered their phones, they were surprised that the prisoner had not come back to prison. That is when it dawned on them that something was wrong. They rushed to Mbella's mother-in-law's house and Mbella was not there. They rushed to the hospital where Mbella was supposed to have gone for check-up, and Mbella was not there either. So they rushed back to the prison. They were arrested and became prisoners like us. Later on it was revealed that Mbella had sold his house and sent his wife and all his children out of the country.

My best time was when we carried out church activities. There were many organisations carrying out evangelisation and other religious activities in prison. In fact, it is a fertile ground for them to carry out humanitarian services. They came with gifts in the form of; food, clothes and toiletries. Their teachings helped us to focus on God and helped take our minds away from our situations. It helped shape our lives and made us God dependent.

The way New Year eve was celebrated in prison was very peculiar. The wake always started with church service as from 10 pm on 31st December. At midnight, you had mixed cries of 'Bonne Année!' and weeping. It seemed as if some abscess got burst and people wanted to cry out the pain.

Women cried for their families and their loved ones left back home. Then, just as the weeping started, it quickly ended and was switched to jubilation. Hash whiskey called Lion D'or and Kitoko surfaced from hiding places and even the warders helped in ensuring that there was enough for everyone who wanted to take it. This ended in drunken sprees associated with dancing and singing. At one point, the prison administration thought they could take matters in their own hands and regulate the amount of whisky consumed that day by providing it. Little did they know that they created a door for the prison to be flooded by Kitoko and Lion D'or.

It's really another world. During cultural or sport activities, you had to see how excited the girls were to go out and meet the boys. It was the same for the men, some of whom would have the pleasure of touching a woman for the first time in a year.

Having a telephone in prison was a big deal. Telephones are forbidden inside prison cells, but almost every female prisoner owned one. Even if originally you did not want a phone, one way or the other, somebody induced you to own one. Warders devised means of making money out of prisoners by conducting abrupt searches to seize the phones. But just as the warders were planning to search, the information would leak, and before they came, all the phones would have disappeared into hiding places.

Hiding places for phones were chiselled on the walls of concrete and plank. Since warders were very cunning, we had to constantly devise new means of hiding the phones.

In prison you find a lot of skilled labour. When I was there a new building was raised using prisoners. There were carpenters, bricklayers, and even architects and electricians among prisoners. In prison, almost every profession and skill is represented. It is indeed the country in miniature.

Normally, you were not supposed to have money more than twenty thousand francs. Any amount higher than that was supposed to be given to the prison administration for safe keeping, and for you to request for it to be given to you in smaller amounts. To avoid that route, given how cunning warders are, we hid our money inside the bonkers that we built inside the beds.

Every year, during the week of 20th May, our national day, they brought a mixed group of student gendarmes, police and warders – those of them who came to Yaoundé for the march pass – to practice how to conduct a search on us. Since the warders did not welcome this invasion of their territory, they made sure that we were warned to send every contraband item in our possession out of prison. The gendarmes almost always pushed the warders aside, because they thought that the warders favoured us. The gendarmes could search the place for one whole day and would not meet a single phone. They ended up picking things like forks and spoons, which of course were given back to us immediately they left.

If keeping some articles would cause me problems I gave them to warders to keep and I collected a week after the search. At one point I had my laptop inside the prison. That was when I was writing my report. They would not permit me to go to the computer room or to the library to write, because I needed to be escorted and this posed a logistical problem. Given the complications involved in going to the library, I just arranged for my laptop to be sent to me in prison and that's how I wrote my defence.

In prison, females cook for themselves, they are not cooked for. I think they tried feeding the females and the females refused to eat the food. If you see what they give the males, it's an insult. When you look at the meal served the males, you can count the number of grains of beans inside the plate of corn. And there is no oil. It is all white like food for pigs. They just take rice, beans or corn and boil without picking it. And it is even the prisoners themselves who do the boiling. So I think they must have tried at one point and realised that women refused to eat. So they gave the women the raw foodstuffs.

Once a month, they give the females raw food; they give us corn, beans, etc. Each person had around 10 cups of corn, and 6 or 7 cups of beans depending on the enrolment at that particular point in time. If the enrolment is low, you will have many more cups of beans and groundnuts. There was also some salt and a bit of palm oil.

Even if they were afraid that allowing us to have kerosene cookers and matches could burn down the place, I think it is something they had to live with. We were not permitted to have gas cookers but only kerosene cookers, even microwaves and grill ovens.

One night one of the rooms caught fire and got burnt. But it was not from a kerosene cooker or because of the match. That night there was a short circuit on one of the beds and the next thing, we just saw fire in the room. When the women started shouting and screaming and knocking, nobody came. A warder stood looking at us and refused to open the gates of the quarters, because he was afraid prisoners might escape out of prison. When the other warders heard our screams, they thought we wanted to distract them from their posts in order to escape. So the warder stood there watching us fighting fire and smoke. The smell of smoke and our shouting finally alerted somebody from the head office who came and opened the gate into the quarters for us to rush out. We could have burnt or suffocated to death. Before the fire-fighters could come from outside, the room was completely burnt and the fire was already extending to other rooms in the quarter.

The worst thing that could happen to you in prison was to take ill at night. During the day the quarters was full of warders, but at night none of them slept there. All of them slept at the head office, which was about 500m from the quarters. We kept on knocking, on the metallic gates, hoping that someone would hear us and come to make enquiries. This was a normal night sound. I carried out deliveries of pregnant women, because the warders were not available. That was something that also struck me in the place.

75

The pregnant women in prison never attended antenatal consultation, and when they went into labour, those who alerted the prison warders early enough were rushed to the Nkoldongo health centre for delivery. These women were rushed back to prison immediately after delivery. With your baby, they brought you back. And they kept you there in that situation. And God is so good. I never saw any of these women suffer. Even those who had been programmed for caesarean sessions end up with normal deliveries while in prison. That was the beautiful miracle I saw there. There was this girl who got into labour, crying and saying that her doctor had said she had to be operated upon. Nothing happened of that sort. She went and had a normal delivery and came back. The prison did not provide any financial assistance for the hospitalised cases. The prisoners paid their own health bills and in most cases since the family members were never around or rich enough to pay these bills, the inmates contributed money for the bills. We were a real community, in every sense of the word.

That said, it is difficult to be a prisoner in this country without a family outside. You are still under the care of your family, even if you are in prison and nothing has been put in place like a health insurance scheme to help prisoners who feel ill. That is why the death rate in prison was very high. Fortunately, in cases of emergencies the inmates and other benevolent and sympathetic persons contributed for the care of these souls. The warders always made sure that they collected their transport money and daily fees out of the money contributed to assist the sick person. It is as if you were begging to be imprisoned.

There is this instance, something happened to me in court. In the fourth year of my imprisonment, it was suddenly decided by the powers that be that the warders were assisting us to leave the court and go to our houses. For this reason, we were escorted to court by the gendarmes and warders.

After court session I wanted to have a brief discussion with my lawyer, which was permitted. While I was still discussing with my lawyer, this gendarme came and asked me to leave. I asked him to let me finish talking with my lawyer. He pushed me away from the lawyer and the lawyer left. I went and collected my bag of food. My God! The next thing I saw, this man lifted me up and I fell on the floor. Not knowing what to do with me, he pulled me from the floor. The state council was called for to witness the scene, although before he could arrive, I was handcuffed and taken back to prison. At the prison gate, he insisted on removing the cuffs but I resisted. Four of them came and held me for him to remove the cuffs. They forced me to take off the hand cuffs because he was going to be reprimanded if I entered the prison with the handcuffs.

The reaction of the warders and even his superiors proved that I was right in resisting having the handcuffs removed. The next day, I was called upon to give a report to the prison authorities and to a captain of the squad. The situation helped the warders to present their frustration to the minister of justice, since they did not like the fact that gendarmes were accompanying us to court. The procurer general called the gendarmerie. The only thing they did is that they changed that gendarme; they said he was never going to escort us again. The next day, the head of that team called for me and apologised, saying I should know that it was the man, that particular man had a problem.

What annoyed this gendarme that day was that during the hearing, one of my colleagues, who took the witness stand, narrated the amount of money he made while he was in service. The gendarmes got angry and grumbled aloud. One said: 'Yes, you people have finished all the money from the government coffers and then I am there working'. Later on, we were told that we provoked them to anger when they listened to us discussing so much money. It felt to them as if we were defending the millions that we were paid illegally. The gendarme who attacked me was said to have been standing there the whole day, his legs were paining and we were there narrating millions that we had buried and we will go and eat with our families.

There is the adage in English 'If you want to hang a dog give it a bad name'. I think that is what happened to some of us who went to Kondengui under 'operation Epervier'. Even the person defending you did not believe in your innocence. Prison inmates did not believe you either. So what about the common Cameroonians on the streets, who feel that their poverty has been worsened by your embezzling greed? How could I convince anyone that some of us were only used as smoke screens to show the outside world that the government was fighting corruption? I hope that the economy has improved and that things have changed for the better with 'operation Epervier'.

I dreamt a lot in prison. It was mostly horrible dreams. I constantly fought in my dreams. The first three years, I constantly fought in my dreams. Curiously, in these dreams, I kept on finding myself in a place at Bomaka, one street in Bomaka. I dream that I was going into a hole, into a house that had no outlet and I would fight and fight and fight and I would get up and pray and say, 'My God, I am not going to stay in this place'. For three good years, I kept on having that particular dream, as well as others. The dreams were too many. Everybody who comes into that place, that's the first thing they have, the dreams. And not good dreams, horrible dreams; you keep on fighting in your dreams. You are either eating in your dreams or being eaten. In some dreams, I am moving in circles round the same place, circling nonstop. But this particular one in Bomaka kept on for a long time. I even asked people outside of prison to pray for me. I said I keep on seeing myself in a particular house, an uncompleted house around Bomaka. I decided to keep a diary of these dreams.

The dreams were bad. But towards the end, the dreams changed. The horrible dreams became fewer and fewer. At one point, there was one of the dreams where I even realised I was somewhere in France and the presidents were up there and I was down in the valley somewhere, sitting on graveyards, not really able to come out from that level down, that place where I was. My dreams were almost entirely about things that happened outside the prison. Rarely did I dream about activities of the prison.

One of my lasting memories of prison is Joey. She was a permanent presence with only flitting moments of absence. To her, prison was home. Even when they released me, she was there. Joey will always come and accompany you, and see you off. And when she is out, she is always around the central post office, doing things almost as if to skim her way back into where she rightly belonged.

When I fought with her over water the day following my arrival in prison, the next day we were friends. She fights with you and the next day she wants food, she wants money. If you don't give it, she insults you. Insolence and belittling talkativeness were her stock in trade. She used her foul mouth to generate food, money and favours for herself. To stop Joey from insulting you, you give Joey money. Joey will be your best friend. But the day that there is no money, Joey will insult you from the top of your head to the toes of your feet. And she will tell everybody useless things about you.

Even if you are round the post office and Joey is free, she is always around there hawking one thing or the other. And she will come and tell you, if you are going around, she says, 'Don't worry. I will warn my people that they should not disturb you, because you are like me.' And when she comes back to prison, she says, 'I saw this person and I was there protecting the person and the person did not even care about me.'

She is very confident about who she is. All the judges in Yaoundé know Joey. They are really tired of Joey. When she is in prison, the mother brings food, fruits and vegetables and she sells. Then the mother comes from outside and collects the money. Joey made us understand that she became what she is today because of the mother, that it is the mother who pushed her into it. It seems as if the mother encouraged her to steal and then the mother collects the money.

Chapter Eight

Something that struck me during my ordeal is that people I thought were very close to me were the very people who went around propagating the story that I had embezzled.

Take the case of the lady who met my daughter in the US and informed her that she heard that in my house, I hid money under the carpet in the parlour. You know how depressing this type of information can be. My daughter had just dropped out of school because she could no longer pay school fees, and somebody was going around spreading rumours about her mother. She least expected such a comment from that lady who passed for a family friend. Another lady who braved the hassle of visiting me in Kondengui actually went back and told people that I was not looking like a prisoner. To her, I wasn't miserable enough.

I heard stories that I was not disturbed since I had kept the money to use after leaving the prison, and that I was never going to work again to earn a living.

When you are in that type of situation people will want to see what they can get out of it. During the early days of my stay in prison, someone went to my home and asked one of the children in my home for my cheque book, claiming that I had asked him to bring the cheque book to me. Interestingly, the man did not know that I could communicate with the children in the house from my prison cell. This child called and asked me whether I had asked for my cheque book to be sent to me through this person. I told her to send the man away very fast, because he was a thief.

Human nature!

This situation made me to be very cautious when I am with so called friends. I even discovered that my own family members only stood by me because blood is thicker than water as the saying goes. I even remember my own sister asking me that if I kept the money somewhere, I should tell them where it was so that they could give it back. That day, I felt hurt more than anything, because I did not expect my own direct relatives to say such a thing.

The next thing I was insulted for was my negligence. 'If you were a good manager, is it possible that you will be signing papers and you don't keep a copy anywhere?' I was repeatedly asked this question, not always in words. In as much as I explained to them, they did not seem to understand. I did not blame them though. It was the pressure from the outside world and what they heard concerning me that pushed them to believe what they could about me.

In Cameroon we have that tendency of saying there is no smoke without fire. So how could I have been arrested if something had not gone wrong? This logic is difficult to beat.

I realised if you are working somewhere and people start really manifesting their hatred towards you, you have to be super careful with them. Live around them like a snake. Be very wise. I thought that maybe my own intelligence and my technical know-how could help me overcome all the hurdles that I was facing. At one point, I even thought that my output was going to speak better for me than all the talks about me.

This is a useless country. I don't even want to hold any duty post again in this country. It's not worth it. Even if I want to hold any duty post, it's going to be for my own enterprise, not for another person's, let alone the state.

People genuinely believed that I had embezzled lots of money, and many of the high officials in the South-West Province kept sniffing around for where I could possibly have invested or banked the money. When they heard that a house was being built somewhere by someone from the North-West Province, the first suspect was me. They combed the banks for accounts that they could link to me, and sent private investigators to my home village as well as my husband's to see if I was erecting storey buildings and mansions overnight. When they still could find nothing directly or remotely connected to me, they declared that I had dug a hole and buried the millions somewhere known only to me.

Had it been that I gave money to the controllers, I would have been spared imprisonment and all the consequences of my imprisonment. In this Cameroon, if you want to be an honest civil servant, maybe you should not hold a duty post. Otherwise, people always expect bribes from you. And the lure of life behind bars is never far away. Quite paradoxically, the good ones are those who go behind bars.

It is believed that the controllers have superior knowledge. The controllers' report in my case was taken for the gospel truth. Even though these gentlemen and lady, I later learnt, were trained as secondary school teachers, civil administrators, statisticians and, etc. None of them had been trained on project management. Here, they controlled a sector they understood nothing about. They came with the notion of the public financing, whilst the programme under which I was working received funds from the World Bank, with its own rules and regulations for accounting and management. They controlled us with notions of the public treasury that we were managing public funds and these funds were supposed to belong to the public treasury. This frustration was repeated over and over by persons controlled by this team who found themselves behind bars. The unfortunate thing was we were behind bars based on a report the controllers had written against us, a report the government was all too keen to use to clean its image with the outside world, by using us as examples. What I used to wonder about was how we could have been kept for so long without judgement and yet the very international world the government was eager to please did not find the legal system wanting.

Here I am today, after the gospel truth of the controllers was declared a lie, but the government did not care that I spent so many years of my life behind bars when its controllers are not the best. Interestingly, the controllers claimed that they were not responsible for our imprisonment, when we accused them of being biased in the report they wrote. According to them, they were asked to control a programme and to produce a report, which they did. Whatever happened to the report thereafter was not their concern. Even when they were in court as witnesses for the state, they defended what they wrote, not caring who was hurt on the way.

I was struck that the Anglophone does not have a say in this country. I was asked to only speak in French. In the Mfoundi high court, I accepted to speak in French because it is a division court. During hearings in the special criminal court, there was nobody on the panel who was English speaking. The presiding judge insisted that I speak in French. Many at times when I even spoke in French, and brought in some words in English, they will turn around and ask me, 'Can you translate that in French?' Here I was, struggling to be heard and defending myself in a foreign language. I felt like a stranger in my own country.

The magistrates in Cameroon are not free. Even before the presiding judge at the special criminal court could pronounce his final judgment, hearing was adjourned to two weeks after. The excuse, according to the presiding magistrate being that, he had written his summary of the case and forwarded it to his hierarchy for approval, and since the hierarchy did not react on time, he had to adjourn the reading of the judgement to a later date. An independent judge would have gone ahead and passed his judgement irrespective of the reaction of hierarchy.

I don't know whether I would like to have anything to do with the judiciary again. If I find any problem that is going to end up in a case, I think I will run without looking behind.

I advise that you should never wish imprisonment even on your worst enemy. I saw men who went to prison as normal people and during the course of the imprisonment went off. They developed mental problems and became mad. It is very traumatising. Some of them ended up being abandoned by relatives and friends. Maybe the wives and children they left behind have taken off to different ways of life. What about women who while in prison hear that not only have their husbands married other wives, but that their children can no longer go to school and have become street children? I even saw a lady who was served divorce papers in prison. That is why I say no one should wish imprisonment on anybody. You should not wish imprisonment on anybody, not even your worst enemy.

To survive prison, I made friends. I made a lot of friends in prison. For five and a half years in prison, if you don't make friends then what? At the end of the day you eat with them, you live with them... At least, you become like a family. Immediately I came out of prison, I had to refocus myself back to the people outside. I had gotten so use to the prison family. Even when I have something to share with someone, I will easily look for somebody who left the prison than looking for somebody who is outside here, because these outsiders, however close they claim to be, will not even understand the angle I am coming from.

I made friends and a lot of my friends have been released. There is Madame Haman. She became like a mother to some of us. Fortunately, she was released one month after I left the place. And even the FEICOM ladies who were released and rearrested, they finally won their case at the Supreme Court and were released. We talk with each other very often. Something can happen and they will always call to find out: 'Have you heard about this?' Like one of the former ministers who died, still awaiting trial, Mr Engoulou. Instances like that will make us to call each other and even organise the funeral and thanking God for his mercy for releasing us.

When I was released, I thought that people were going to receive me just the way I was before I went inside. But I realised that when I am coming towards people with an open mind, I see people shutting up. In meetings and social gatherings I used to attend prior to prison, when I come in these days, the people with whom I even used to joke and socialise, I see them being very evasive, pretending to welcome me while being very distant. I can sit there and leave without even talking to anybody. You know they are looking at you... wrestling with their thoughts and their stereotypes having the better of them. I go to church, I feel free, but you realise that people are funny around you. They want you to make a statement about prison. It's fun to me. Only people who are really open-minded still look at me to be the same person. But ninety percent of people look at me differently. I remember going to buy meat and complaining about the scale the butcher was using, only for him to retort: 'Is that what you went and learnt in prison, to come and be correcting me outside here?'

At work when they are talking about the prison and I am around, you see people who know my status, very uncomfortable. Those who are very bold will present me as an example of injustice in Cameroon – how I went to prison and some people who embezzled are still outside. In fact, I look at the larger society as comedians. You want people to be punished for your own ills.

When you have been to prison and back, it seems as if the real prison is the society outside with all its prejudices. I now understand why many people who leave prison want to change town to go and start life elsewhere where a lot of people do not know them. People who used to live in Yaoundé, will leave and go to Douala, just to be away from the judging eyes of those with whom they are familiar. I hate that when people look at me they do so with a lot of pity. I am the very human being I was before prison, so why should somebody pity me? There is nothing wrong with me.

That is one of the reasons why I went to Nigeria and stayed for two months after I was released. I just wanted to leave this environment with the pitying and just to be somewhere else. It is very stigmatising. – 'Oh, this is an ex-convict; this is one who was in prison and all that.'

Ironically, immediately we were arrested, the funding for the particular programme that we were running dwindled and finally ended. The progress report was very positive. The funders themselves came and saw that everything was good. They wrote a report telling the Cameroon government that there was no mismanagement of the funds, and congratulating the team that the government had arrested and imprisoned for mismanagement. It was a paradox that the Cameroon government, the beneficiaries themselves, turned around and arrested the very people who had been managing the programme. The funders of the project were perplexed. Either they were very wrong or we running the programme very wrong. Someone somewhere was not serious. So they stopped the funding. Unable to fund the programme itself, the Cameroon government has not been able to maintain it.

Roughly two months after I was released from prison, the provincial delegate of health who had resisted my appointment died. Nobody expected that I was going to go for his funeral, but I went there. The widow got up and came and embraced me and said 'Doctor eh, Doctor!' I sought to comfort her in her grief.

When I was making my thanksgiving, I invited all of my former colleagues who used to write all sorts of negative reports about me, but none of them showed up. When I am somewhere, when any of them sees me, they take another direction. Perhaps because they know they were misguided. Just the other day, one of them was standing in front of the cold store at the entrance to my house. I don't know where she was going to, but as I parked my car and was coming out, she quickly halted the first taxi that was coming and jumped inside. I have become like a juju to a lot of them.

There is one of my drivers whom I disciplined and then finally fired out of the project. I asked him to take me to Kribi, and he refused to accompany me, preferring to drive the service car that I had assigned him around town, doing little or nothing. He told me to my face that he was not going to Kribi. He was part of the machinations at the office. I made my way to Kribi and back by other means, but when I returned and fired him, he took his pen, wrote and reported me to Yaoundé that I have removed him from service. He also reported me to other influential figures locally, who accused me of dismissing locals and employing people from the North-West Province. That was far from the truth, as the driver I hired to replace the recalcitrant one was a local Bakweri man from Bokwai. Bad faith was their prized currency.

Chapter Nine

Many years have gone by since my ordeal in Kondengui Central prison. Life goes one. I am okay. The wound is healed. The scar expressed by my memory is taking longer to heal but I believe it will eventually fade away.

Looking back, I think I survived the Kondengui ordeal because I went through a boarding school. Inside the boarding school, you meet children who come from all types of families. I was able to fit into life at Kondengui because of this. I could cope with those who were out to fight, the jealous ones, the gossips and many other challenging categories of people, just because of the experience I had had in boarding school.

Even the type of discipline that the warders thought they were meting out on me, perhaps thinking they were doing something that I had never ever seen before, was all déjà-vu. The discipline I encountered in boarding school throughout my 7 years in St Augustine's College, equipped me perfectly for life in prison. From secondary school to high school, the reverend sisters, the reverend fathers and the, prefects, amongst the students, were all about discipline. So having someone command, instruct and demand total obedience was something I was used to. There was nothing new in being told what to do or how to behave.

The only difference is that at boarding school, I had an objective to attain. I had an education that I was after. In Kondengui I was living in limbo.

In boarding school discipline pushes you to fulfil yourself, whereas in Kondengui, it is discipline that punishes.

Prison is discipline for discipline sake. I don't think that's the type of discipline I want. Take for example a warder who will smuggle in a telephone for you to use and then come afterwards for that telephone that he himself brought in, merely because he is looking for money. And when you refuse to give the phone or the money, you are sanctioned. How can one call that discipline? To me it is not discipline. All I see is enclosure and that is it. But what I had in secondary school helped me.

And then the fact that I also came from a background that was religious also helped. My father, of blessed memory, was a teacher training teacher for the Baptists. This association with the Baptists gave me a strong foundation in religion. In prison, I immediately warmed up to all the religious people around there. I embraced them fully as something I could identify with from childhood.

Religion helped me a lot in prison, and I came out of there a better person. Today I even tell people that to be a better person, they should go to Kondengui. Having had my patience tested to the limit in prison, what annoyance could I possibly find out here that I haven't experienced in there? When I meet people shouting or trying to dramatize their importance or capacity to harm others, I just, with disarming calm, ask them: 'what's your problem?' I no longer find anything that makes me tense and angry. It's all déjà-vu. I tend to laugh and walk away when someone attempts to upset or pick a quarrel with me. I wonder whether I am still the same person.

I have been through the hardest place, through the most hardened criminals, persons who take pleasure in hurting others. I think I outgrew the anger that I used to have before I went to prison.

Yesterday I was in church, we went for a wedding. A man comes and blocked the gate saying we are too late to enter the church. I turned and looked at him.

I said, 'Are you normal? Do you know why I left Buea to come to Limbe?'

He said, 'madam, the activity was supposed to start at 2 o'clock, you cannot come at 2:30 and expect to enter the church. Moreover, the priest has started preaching.'

I said, 'Do you know that that priest is preaching for me?'

The man was adamant.

I turned. People were grumbling and everything. I faced the man and said, 'You are not God, this is God's house. If you think that I am going to get my ticket to Heaven through you, you are wasting your time.' I opened the door and went in.

This man followed me into the church, wanting to create a scene. I sat. I said nothing. He insisted I must leave the church. I asked him, 'You know where I came from?

He shook his head.

'I came from Kondengui, and if you continue, I will climb on that altar and tell the priest that you are disturbing.'

The man took off very fast.

This is an example of the type of issues over which I would work myself up so much. Before Kondengui, I would have asserted myself by relentlessly pushing and asking: 'Do you know whom you have to deal with? But now, when you bring yourself low I am at that level. When you're high up there, I am also at that level. It might sound strange to a lot of people, but I think I came out from that place, behaviour and character wise, a better person. That said, I wouldn't wish prison on anyone simply because prison would likely make them a better person. But I'm saying that if you have character problems, if you have problems with anger, go there, go, you will be treated.

If you used to have anger tantrums, you go to that prison, they will solve that anger for you. I am talking about anger in particular. Somebody will come to provoke that anger out of

91

you, to see how far you can go. They are measuring the level of your anger with theirs. I have the impression that they equate anger with strength. When they provoke that anger and you react, you end up in a fistfight. At the end of the day, you will see where you are, where you stand as far as your anger is concerned, and as far as your strength is concerned. But if you are somebody who reasons well, at one point, you will ask yourself is it really worth the pain. So when they provoke you at times, you just turn and look at them and laugh and smile. And as the provocations continue, at one point it means nothing to you. Whether they throw water or insults at you, you smile and you go your way. That's what I mean about the capacity of the prison to change you positively. Otherwise, I don't think that prison is really there to bring anything good out of anybody.

In boarding secondary school, the reverend sisters had an objective to build better characters. The people in prison might claim that they are out to build better characters as well, that they discipline with the intent to correct. They think by disciplining they are correcting. But I wonder whether the bad things they are doing to inmates would match the good things done by the reverend sisters that we could complain about but hardly fault. In college, the sisters will guide you and tell you, 'please don't do this again.' It was my personal strength of character that resulted in my coming out of prison a better person. A lesser person may not go and come out a better person. Some innocent persons have gone into prison and come out being hardened criminals. If you are not careful, you will mix with the wrong people. I think it is all down to the mind-set of the person.

What you use an anchor while in prison makes all the difference. If I went there with nothing to hold on to, I may not have survived. I had a family to hold on to. I had a daughter to hold on to. I kept on thinking about my family outside. The question I held in my mind was, will I want them to come and meet me in this place another person from what they expected of me? If you don't have that in mind, you will want to follow what the other prisoners are doing. You will come out worse than what you were before.

The prison has a very strong capacity to change anyone. Even the warders, they end up as prisoners of prisoners for their pockets. There are many warders who depend on prisoners for their livelihood. There are warders who are actually like houseboys or house girls to some of those very rich prisoners. The phones warders smuggle in for a fee are used to summon the very same warders to come and render services in exchange for payment. Those who have warders at their beck and call can make them run around like cockroaches doing their bidding. If that is not being a prisoner to a prisoner, I don't know what it is. It's certainly not doing your duty as a warder. That is not what a warder is supposed to do. But they have become like houseboys and house girls to some of the rich prisoners. And to imagine some of the mean things that they go around doing! They are so mean!

It is easy to buy your freedom in prison and even out of it. If I and others I know had not been Paul Biya's prisoners, it would certainly have been possible for us to equally buy our way out of the place. From a warder – never mind a magistrate – you can buy your right to freedom. I know a lot of prisoners who did that. You pay an amount every month and you are free to leave the prison premises and go out into the city for the whole day. And in some instances, they only return to prison around or well after midnight, and by 5 a.m. they are all gone again. It's something very normal, and even though the gendarmerie nearby has staged arrests many times, the practice is rife. Despite the repeated arrests of prisoners leaving prisoning, little has changed. The gendarmes have given up. Only once in a while when they realise that it's too much, they will conduct some arrests. Otherwise, they have given up. The gendarmerie are also complicit. When they arrest the prisoners, they receive their own part of the money and they free the prisoners, who return to doing exactly the same thing soon after. For the warders, it is easy come, easy go money.

Apart from anger management and resisting provocation, I have also moved on in several other regards since I was released. I am back to my house as the mother. I have resumed my place inside my family. I am the sister, the mother, the aunty to my many nieces and nephews. I think I have regained the position I once occupied. Members of my family look upon me as a force to be reckoned with. When they have their problems, their issues, they call and I respond in one way or the other. I counsel them the way I can and where I can give assistance, I give them the assistance. And to my mother, she has received her daughter back and she is very happy with that. When we have any activity in the family, now she will be very happy to see me by her side. I am really like the prodigal daughter, the lost but found daughter. In general, it was been so far so good. Relations with my family are good. When they call, we talk with each other and I listen. They respect my opinion just as I respect theirs.

Once in a while, when I get provoked and I want to shut people up, I make them aware that they are talking to a former prisoner. I notice I gain some respect when I do that. People turn and look whenever I draw attention to that fact. I can hear them asking themselves wide-eyed and in the perplexed silence, 'Is she for real? And if I continue, am I sure she's not going to become the real criminal?' Being an ex-convict and making it known opens doors and earns respect. Every now and then, I feel I could do with both. Otherwise jobwise, as I said, I've moved on.

After leaving the prison, the Cameroon government, as usual, behaved as if nothing happened. After one year of moving up and down, I was finally re-absorbed into the civil service. That was after I applied for a job, wrote a test and passed, and attended an interview in the ministry. I attended an interview and I was selected to be in charge of planning, monitoring and evaluation for the national programme for combatting maternal, new-born and child mortality. I went to the programme and I thought this was some top job that I was going to like. But when I received the posting decision, I knew there and then that this government will never change.

Although they made me apply for the job, write the tests, undergo an interview and it was clear I was really the first; after everything, they gave me a posting decision, saying that on this day I have been posted by the minister of public health to be in this programme. I worked with them for a year. We did a beautiful piece. With my knowledge as project manager, we really did a beautiful piece of job. We started the programme from scratch and after working for a year, I turned 55 years old and I had to be retired in line with the regulations of the Cameroon public service. I went and saw the minister and I asked him what next. After spending six years doing nothing, I thought that at least I was going to be considered and given some preferential treatment. The minister encouraged me to write an application for exemption and bring, promising to follow up and send them to the presidency. He said he was sure that they are going to keep me in the administration.

Excited, I compiled the documents, hurriedly did everything and submitted them. But my excitement did not last, as the subdirector who received the documents said to me: 'Even if the minister said it, so what?' Later, I gathered it was a strategy to give me false hope. The minister will pamper you, he does not want you to disturb him. But he has given instructions to the subdirector that when any document comes, 'If I don't give you the go-ahead, don't treat it.' I realised that this man did not want me to continue within the civil service and these particular projects, they were threatening they will not keep me until I had the document signed.

Retirement at the Ministry of Health is hardly as straightforward as it might appear. It's not all medical doctors who retire at 55. That medical profession is very interesting. We have some of them who belong to the higher education sector and even the lowest of them will retire at 60. And even those who end up being professors will retire at 65. Now, I hear they want to go to 70. And then within the Ministry of Health, we have those of them like us who belong solely under the Ministry of Health. Even then, all the directors belong to the Ministry of Higher Education, as a way of avoiding early retirement.

Those without a connection with higher education feel beleaguered. That's the problem. When you start talking to them, they look at it as if you're disturbing. They sit there, they don't do the work. They don't do the work for the ministry of health. They are neither doing the work for higher education, nor are they doing work for health. They simply want to guarantee that it takes as long as possible before they go on compulsory retirement.

What do you expect of a Ministry of Health where even the person in charge of personnel, is a secondary school teacher? The man in charge of human resources presently is a secondary school teacher. Knowing nothing about health, how can he empathise with the plight of the medical corps? It means nothing to him and the rest who go shopping for prolongation services elsewhere in higher education, whether we go or we stay, it means nothing to them. The whole government and public service is sick. I'm out of it. I'm happy I'm out of it.

When I sensed that neither the minister nor the subdirector was interested in keeping me a day longer than necessary, I started looking for other jobs. And as God will have it, on the very day I was supposed to retire, I was called up for my current job. I am working for Elizabeth Glazer Paediatric Foundation. It's an American NGO that fights paediatric AIDS. They are based in Africa, Asia and elsewhere in the developing countries. I'm working as a site assistant in the Limbe Regional Hospital, where I organise trainings in paediatric care, the idea being to build a centre of excellence at the hospital. When I will finish building the centre for excellence, then we will be bringing doctors from elsewhere to be trained in that hospital. It's very challenging. Funded by PEPFA under CDC Atlanta, this is the first project of its kind in Cameroon. As a first, each and every one of us working with the programme are groping our way through, but with increased consultation, we are setting the pace for future employees to build on once we yield fruit. I find it very interesting. Jobwise, that is how I am and that is how I found myself back here in the South West region.

I've passed through a lot of trauma, a lot of issues that make me realise that I need to have strong will power to achieve what I want. I don't easily give up. That is something I'm discovering. I did not think I had it before. Originally, everybody will tell me 'Ah, you're that type of person when you get discouraged you just abandon'. I realised that maybe words like that just kept on making me see that I had to be focused on what I wanted in life.

That's how I even became a medical doctor. I remember this teacher in high school, who kept telling me that I was too short to become a medical doctor. The first time he told me that, we were doing practicals in the laboratory. He said, 'What will you want to be tomorrow?' I said I wanted to be a medical doctor. He said, 'do you think you can become a medical doctor as short as you are?' I said, 'Mr Berinyuy, I will shock you.' There are some things that you say without thinking, and later on you use it like a challenge. I said I will shock you. And from that day, I started convincing myself that I am going to become that medical doctor which my teacher believed I couldn't be on account of my height. So when I left high school, I had the opportunity to go to the Higher Teachers Training School in Bambili. I rejected it. I said I have to be a medical doctor. And that is how I worked towards it. If I'm not challenged, I can let it go. But when someone tells me, 'I don't think you can do it', that's when I will try to prove that I can do it.

There are times when I am too strict to a fault. That's one of my problems. When I know I am doing what is right and you want to derail me, I do everything in my power to resist. It's not as if I did not know where to go and collect the justification documents, but the way I saw it, it was not my responsibility to give them the justification documents. So they should not insist on asking me to give it to them. If there is anything that I regret today, it is my rigidity. A lot of people have described me as being rigid. When you define rules, say I'm in charge of this, this other person is in charge of this, I respect that and expect everyone else to do same. Immediately you've told me this is what I'm supposed to do, don't expect that I will start changing rules and doing things differently. Had it been that I yielded a bit or I bended or I accepted to just bend a bit to what they wanted, I'm sure I was not going to end up where I ended up. But I thought it was not my business, I had nothing to do there. That is really what got me there.

98

Printed in the United States
By Bookmasters